This Bloodless Liberty

This Bloodless Liberty

Congress' 10 lies that are destroying America —
and how We The People can reclaim
our currency, Constitution, liberty,
and way of life

DAVID M. ZUNIGA

a part of Salem Communications
Longwood, FL
www.xulonpress.com

Dedicated to mom, Patricia Zuniga, in glory; aunt Norma Benavides, for Christian norms and nobility; cousin Norma Hunt, for unmerited lovingkindness; Stephanie, first birth I witnessed and smitten ever since; David Jr., beloved son for whom I hope in Christ; Garfield, whom I'm honored to call brother and son; our grandchildren, my treasures; my AmericaAgain! team for such dedication; Bruce, Carlos, Keith and Kurt, for being my friends; Jemmy Madison for designing it, and Larry Kramer for opening the box; William Shakespeare for life's words; Kurt Bestor, Keith Green, Fernando Ortega, and Ralph Vaughan Williams for its music; my brother Oscar, for everything; Sylvia, my Proverbs 31 woman these 33 years. Above all, to the Christ –

Ruler over every world, birthing countless more
in vasty pillars and caves of far nebulae.
Things that impress (terrorize!) us, are nothing to You
by Whom all things are made.

We abide this present earth, this fiction,
reality being far beyond our feeble minds;

We fell!
(Fall daily still.)

What dream is this – Creator dies, redeeming creatures?
For time-bound dreamers, this alone is real;
our mortal shackles (time and sin) compounding mystery.

Answers finally dawn – true life begins – only when
our shell has run its course:
We fall...

We rise!

O High King, I long to see Your face, forever.

Contents

Chapter 1
Introduction

I would seek unto God, And unto God would I commit my cause...
He frustrateth the devices of the crafty so that their hands
cannot perform their enterprise. He taketh the wise
in their own craftiness... (Job 5:8,12,13)

Those...who pay no regard to religion and sobriety in the persons
whom they send to the legislature...are guilty of the greatest absurdity
and will soon pay dear for their folly. (John Witherspoon)

The tombstone of a civilization is laid at that point where truth is no longer defended because it cannot be known. No civilization is eternal; each has a discernible birth, leaves an historical record, and then dies with a whimper or a bang.

In some cases, the whimpering can span centuries; witness the jackals of Islam picking at Europe's dry bones today. Rather than defend their citizens and cultures, the European governments that once were imperial predators across the world are now content to use their own citizens as carrion.

The predator instinct is just one aspect of fallen humanity. Beginning in the Lincoln era, government has increasingly and ever more audaciously preyed on us. We suffer regulation, invasion of privacy, and taxation from school boards to Washington D.C., not to mention countless bites in between. Half of America seems on the take or on the dole. The New World now exceeds the Old World corruption that our founders risked their lives to escape.

A time of great hope

Having said that, this book will demonstrate that as unlikely as it may appear, we have more reason for hope today than in the past two centuries. Truth *can* be known; if it's defended, we have hope.

I will not attempt to expose every illegal or immoral act of our government over the past 150 years; *Suggested Reading* at the end of the book will point you to further reading on that score. This is a call to lifelong action and a lawful, practical plan for that action, that you can join today. This book is for Americans like me, who have had enough and who want to take America back.

I'll propose a new way of relating to government: not politics, elections, or even secession. Not more faxes, petitions, or pink slips delivered to predators. Such campaigns have transformed hucksters into millionaires, but wrought no change in government. Instead, we must begin to perform our citizen duty assigned by the founding fathers.

The buck stops with *you*

This book will demonstrate that America's plight is *our* fault; We The People[1] are apex sovereigns over our Constitution. We don't look to employees to reform themselves; we use our retained power of oversight and law enforcement. To get America back, we must *take* it back rather than appealing to party machines. We must graduate from politics in our lives; employ house-by-house, coordinated tactical wisdom; stop squandering family time.

The internet provides us the best opportunity in 200 years to reclaim lost liberty. No population has ever used the internet to stop government corruption and re-establish rule of law. Because of our Constitution, we're the only population on earth who can peacefully achieve this in the foreseeable future. This book will demonstrate how AmericaAgain! can be one way to do it.

First, I must debunk ten lies that federal Leviathan has used to enslave us. Then I will present the AmericaAgain! tactical plan. At *www.MyAmericaAgain.org* the AmericaAgain! Declaration appears in full, and is also reproduced as Appendix C hereto.

Our plan follows James Madison's work. It is lawful, moral, and logistically simple. Now don't say that no one has offered an action plan to recover the life and republic that we once had.

Seven generations in the desert

Why have productive Americans been incapable of arresting the lawlessness that we so clearly despise? In Chapter 12, you will see how massive the parasite segment is, and how it is banking on you remaining ignorant, too perplexed to take action. The two producing generations today have not recognized the predators; nor do their children, now in K-12 schools. Nor did the four generations during the 20th century, including the 'greatest generation' that is more socialist than any other. We certainly cannot win a battle if we don't even know who our enemies are.

The ancient tradition of governments plundering citizens is very well described by economics professor Joseph Salerno in the introduction to Murray Rothbard's classic on American banking:

> The State throughout history has been a segment of the population that forsakes peaceful economic activity to constitute itself as a ruling class (that) makes its living parasitically by establishing a permanent hegemonic or political relationship between itself and the productive population. This political relationship permits the rulers to subsist on the tribute or taxes routinely and 'legally' expropriated from the income and wealth of the producing class. The latter class is composed of the subjects or, in the case of democratic states, the taxpayers who earn their living through

the peaceful economic means of production and voluntary exchange. In contrast, constituents of the ruling class may be thought of as tax-consumers who earn their living through the coercive political means of taxation of the sale of monopoly privileges.[2]

Unfortunately, Professor Salerno omits the larger portion of the iceberg that plunders productive Americans: the consultants, suppliers, contractors, and many other private-sector beneficiaries of government expenditure. Making up 40% of our population, the predator and parasite sector produces only invoices, tickets, fines, fees, studies, reports, returns, and other burdens for the productive population of America; or it makes 'money' out of thin air and keystrokes, growing fat on the interest.

This is our *domestic* enemy that for six generations has posed a clear and present danger to America. As no foreign enemy could have done, this sector has helped Leviathan to eviscerate our rule of law, kill our currency, burden families to the breaking point, and render private business and personal privacy all but impossible.

Sheepdogs and Taxspenders

To restore the constitutional limits of government, a critical mass of citizens must begin to act as America's sheepdogs; first understanding basics, then taking constructive actions to restore the republic, and finally assuring that the regained ground is secure.

Sheepdogs will recognize the longstanding *domestic* competition between productive and parasitic citizens. They'll be aware of the massive private supplier layer that, like the portion of an iceberg below the waterline, is much larger than government and because it is hidden, more threatening to our liberties and family economy.

Politics attracts an inordinate percentage of slothful and dishonest people. Political parasites – *Taxspenders* – have incentive to keep the Taxpayer hosts confused, ignorant, and satisfied with bread and circuses. Once we grasp these facts of life and begin to think

Taxspender when we meet public- or private-sector parasites, this very un-American game may begin to turn.

Look out America, here comes the world

Besides this domestic parasite sector burdening the productive population, we face increased foreign competition as explained in the modern classic *Empire of Debt:*

> Never before, since the beginning of the industrial revolu-
> tion 300 years ago, have there been so many people outside
> the Western world ready, willing, and able to compete with
> us. Never before have they had so much available capital.
> While Americans spend all their money – and then some,
> the average Chinese worker saves more than 20 percent of all
> he earns. There are more engineers in the city of Bangalore,
> India, than there are in the state of California. They work
> well and cheaply, taking home an average annual pay of
> about $6,000.[3]

Americans must realize that the rest of the world will now com-
pete with us in every area. As we did for centuries, Americans can
hold our own with any other economy on earth in a fair competition, but not while carrying a load of predators and parasites on
our backs. America was designed to reward individual industry and
frugality; not opulence, socialism, or fascism.

Classical fascism: human lions vs. gazelles

Contempt for law is now exhibited by every predator from the
bent city bureaucrat to the corrupt senator, but those who believe
that our disaster began with the progressive era are mistaken.

Although it is more brazen today than ever, Washington D.C.
corruption is a *very* old game. The last president to resist potential
fascist plunder was Andrew Jackson, who used his bully pulpit as

the presidential *horizontal* check-and-balance in 1836 to convince citizens to stop evil bankers.

But presidents are easily bought. The framers believed, and history proves, that we cannot depend on them as subjects depend on their monarch. Our duty is to use our *vertical* check-and-balance power to enforce the Constitution; as Ben Franklin suggested, they gave us "a republic...if you can keep it".

We have failed to keep it for many generations, and so now we resemble a European bureaucratic state, with criminals in the wheelhouse, steering our ship for the rocks, as the U.S. Supreme Court ruled generations ago in *Olmstead v. United States:*

> Our government is the potent, the omnipresent teacher. For good or for ill, it teaches the whole people by its example. Crime is contagious. If the government becomes a lawbreaker, it breeds contempt for law.

Beyond being illegal according to our Constitution, fascism and socialism have failed throughout history. Economics is 10% math and 90% ethics; given man's sin nature, we should not be surprised that socialism has never succeeded. It incentivizes laziness and bureaucracy. Yet many Americans today display a decidedly socialist mindset and emotional response on this subject.

Then there is fascism, which changes the emotional landscape at an even more fundamental level. By definition, *fascism* is the alliance of a police state and corporations, to prey on the People. Despite their ad campaigns, realize that the government and corporations work for you exactly as a lion 'works for' gazelles.

The coming rewards for courage and diligence

However angry we may be at this cruel arrangement, cheers of *"I want action, now!!"* are not the wisest way to deal with predators. Gazelles must learn to think and work together to make a sturdy, reuseable trap for the lions, that can also nab hyenas and jackals who share the lions' kill from the edge of the tree line.

One of my favorite scenes in the movie Braveheart is that in which the disconsolate child William Wallace stands alone at the fresh grave of his father and brother. Uncle Argyll rides up on his huge white warhorse and dismounting, asks the lad what he wants to do. *"I want to kill English,"* replies young Wallace.

Looking down with compassion in his one good eye and a crooked smile on his war-scarred face, Argyll replies, "First we teach you to use *this,"* (pointing to the lad's head) "before we teach you to use *this"* (pulling his long blade from its sheath).

I was classically educated until university; then as an adult I helped to plan, staff, and launch four classical Christian schools in Iowa, North Carolina, and Texas. In addition to the usual subjects, students in these schools also study Latin, logic, debate, rhetoric of composition and oratory, the Great Books of Western civilization, and more. Very handy weapons, just now.

The great benefit in good education is that one learns to think; and the great benefit in a Christian worldview is that one learns to take joy in the economics and physics of God's universe. One learns that prayer avails much, as does hard work. As does tactical thinking. One derives joy in the fact that ideas have consequences soon or late. One learns the tactical value of timing in history.

Seemingly in another life, I was an engineer designing buildings; analyzing structures and their failures, appreciating the certitude of cause-effect, of function-dysfunction. This is another handy weapon; it gives me the opposite view of that held by the conservative celebrities, who are now predicting America's demise.

True, the predators presently appear to enjoy the upper hand. They've been on something of a binge since FDR, and having an absolute *orgy* during Clinton, the Bushes, Obama, and the past few congresses. But I believe that history suggests we are witnessing *the end of their feast, not the beginning.*

More than two million children are being trained at home in America, a phenomenon second only to the internet in its capacity to revive liberty, spiritual and intellectual health, and the rule of law by giving individuals access to truth.

A distant second best is the private education institution; the largest classical Christian school association alone is now boasting 33,000 students. Together, these two movements are feeding thousands of well-trained minds into study of business, law, and professions; they are writing books, hosting blogs, composing and performing magnificent music and art, launching businesses, and becoming expert craftsmen.

An estimated 67 million Americans are non-filers and law-abiding Nontaxpayers, and embargo is a 100% successful solution against predators. A sort of 'family secession', cutting off the enemy's supply at least from one family. *The gazelles have a solution.*

As described in Chapter 12, now comes AmericaAgain! – the first practical, lawful, tactically powerful solution for the productive citizen to resist and even help to end the vast predator-parasite sector. Although this constitutional power has always been ours, the internet now gives us tools for home-based oversight and for unprecedented tactical citizen force-massing.

AmericaAgain! will do what corporations and powerful men have been doing for centuries – force Congress to do our will. The difference is that 'our will' is simply the Constitution; they will obey it, or serve time in their State prison. *The very old game is turning.*

Our ancient legal heritage

What is now the fifty States of the American Republic were once colonies of Britain, Spain, and France, with Roman Catholic positive law tradition losing out to English common law.

Our rule of law did not begin here, of course. It was shaped at its foundations by English law and Christian ethics, perhaps since the Dooms of Aethelberht in the sixth century, but surely by Magna Carta in 1215 A.D., when kings became subject to law for the first time, no longer being a law in themselves, by power.

The longest-lasting constitutional government in history, our ancient rule of law now hangs by a thread. But millions of us are angry and motivated to take up our abdicated duties. Our republic needn't be doomed; truth can still be known and even successfully defended by a minority of the productive American population.

Despite flaws, a magnificent Law

James Madison, in a class by himself among the founders, is one of the least heralded, yet was a 5'-4", 120-pound giant. In his letters to Thomas Jefferson, in his articles for The National Gazette, in those of the Federalist Papers that came from his pen, and in his Virginia Resolutions, Madison was always clear: ultimate power in our government is forever vested in the People.

We The People was the most divinely inspired phrase in the history of human government. Here, Madison informed the world that America's citizens birthed a federal government via sovereign States. Retaining the apex sovereign position over our States, which are sovereign over our federal creation, We The People then divided power among three federal branches.

Per Article I, senators were elected by the legislatures of the States; congressmen elected by their constituents through popular election. This gave the sovereign People and sovereign States each a vote through which they could control Congress. The Senate was designed as the more deliberative voice of State legislatures; the House of Representatives was the more reactive body, reflecting citizen passions of the day.

Per Article II, presidents are chosen by the Electoral College, a representative body of delegates from the States. The popular vote serves in most elections as a seconding vote.

Per Article III, the U.S. Supreme Court hears cases that involve one or more States, or that involve a citizen's claim that his constitutional rights have been usurped by State or federal government; also, after *Marbury v. Madison* in 1803, cases alleging that a State law is unconstitutional.

These are the Constitution's *horizontal* checks-and-balances; the higher-order control is the *vertical* check-and-balance that we have as creators over our federal creature. If there is one concept that you must grasp from this little book, it is this: as a citizen, you have the highest power of government within our Republic, and this *popular sovereignty* carries a heavy responsibility, far beyond voting.

Corruption's pig-in-a-python

A critical vertical check was stripped away in the infamous year 1913 at the hands of the 63rd Congress, which resembled today's 111th Congress in brazen disregard for law. Many of the corrupt players were holdovers from the 61st and 62nd Congresses but by 1913, the money powers were able to elect a religious milquetoast to the White House. In Europe as among the powerful families of America, lions' bellies rumbled. It was time for the hunt.

As has always been the case by the very nature of the machine, the puppets in Congress did as directed. They granted the world's largest counterfeiting concession by enacting the Federal Reserve Act of 1913. The War to Enslave the States[4] had already consolidated power in Washington, D.C. by crushing the insurgent sovereign States. God's justice against an inhuman institution was shrewdly used by the mercantilists, whose allegiance is to mammon.

Lincoln's war and the creation of a new national military force was the first shoe to drop for D.C. Leviathan. Working diligently in the shadows for decades before, by 1913, the mercantilists who had pined for coast-to-coast control of America finally dropped the second shoe, the Sixteenth and Seventeenth Amendments, further enslaving the People and States.

Incidentally, as Appendix D explains, the Seventeenth was the more destructive of the two amendments. The Seventeenth, which AmericaAgain! will work to abolish, was sold as a remedy for undecided Senate elections.

On occasions when no Senate candidate won a plurality in his State legislature's polling, the Senate seat remained vacant and the

State's representation in the Senate diminished by half. We propose a simple solution in the AmericaAgain! Declaration, because the Amendment cured nothing; if a legislature can fail to produce plurality winners, a popular vote can, as well. That political ploy was designed to emasculate the States; to make it so that the People would directly elect congressmen *and* senators, destroying a key facet of the U.S. Constitution's unique design.

Having lost their vote in Congress and their deliberative check on its actions, it was only a matter of time before State legislatures fell in line for federal handouts. Statesmen gave way to politicians, easily bought off with federal largesse that could be divided up with State employees, consultants, special interest groups, cities and counties, school districts, and others who could ensure re-election.

This is the life called politics. Whether for the seat-holder, the bureaucrat or the party functionary, one finds his lifetime career under the bright lights, in the newspapers, on the internet.

This is not new; it harks back to ancient Rome – or in nature, to a thousand grassy clearings across the African plain on any given night, as the coppery smell of warm blood mingles with the sweat, snarls, and recriminating glances from carrion-eaters at the edge of the fray. Politics is blood sport.

The duty of the sovereign citizen

The brilliance of our form of government emanates from a New Testament principle, that God deals not with groups, but with the heart of the individual, holding sinners individually accountable.

God blesses a person when the individual decides to do right, even against fashions, friends, or conventional wisdom. A person's new heart eventually inspires his family and circle of friends. This is the bottom-up process by which God civilizes all of mankind; reformation begins with individual decisions.

Politics perverts this; instead of doing the right thing when it hurts, it beckons you to its projects, programs, and promises; trains the politician to speak to you in mellifluous tones as he runs his traps; trains the People to follow, posters in hand.

As wicked as it is, We The People abdicated our duties first. We must show State governments the way forward, by example.

The meaning of federal republic

Madison put ultimate power in the People, cutting the Gordian knot that had plagued America under Articles of Confederation. The brilliance of the new Constitution was its republican form; a *foedus* or federation between sovereign States made up of sovereign individuals willing to take risks for reward. Americans were willing to work for property, to bleed for liberty, and to always hold God above man; a central state was *never* a part of America's plan.

To avoid Leviathan's return, Madison used a *foedus,* a Roman word meaning a defensive league; this is the meaning of *federal* – precisely the opposite of a powerful central state. Even Alexander Hamilton, a strong proponent of a powerful central government, recognized in Federalist #28 that the People required a flexible *foedus* for defense against tyranny:

> The whole power of the proposed government is to be in the hands of the representatives of the People. This is the essential...security for the rights and privileges of the People...(I)f the representatives of the People betray their constituents, there is no resource left but...self-defense...
> (T)he larger the American population would become, the more effectively we can resist federal government tyranny... provided the citizens understand their rights and are disposed to defend them. The natural strength of the people in a large community, in proportion to the artificial size of the government, is greater than in a small... .

In a sort of warranty language, Hamilton asserts in Federalist #28 that citizens can use our State government when the federal becomes tyrannical, or federal government against overbearing State power. In either case, the People will control:

> Power being almost always the rival of power, the general government will…stand ready to check the usurpations of State governments, and these will have the same disposition towards the general government. The People, by throwing themselves into either scale, will infallibly make it preponderate…. State governments will…afford complete security against invasions of the public liberty by the national authority…they can at once adopt a regular plan of opposition…combine all the resources of the community. They can readily communicate with each other in the different States, and unite their common forces for the protection of their common liberty.

Obviously, Mr. Hamilton was overly optimistic about State governments. He could not have foreseen the financial crime since 1913 by which federal mafia skims $4 trillion annually to buy State legislators whose duty is to restrain our federal creature, and certainly not to eat from its dish.

A false god walking on earth

We have failed to see this abdication because political parties are able to keep donkeys and elephants at one another's throats. Party machines divide, conquer, fleece, and brainwash citizens to see voting as the only, the ultimate exercise of citizen power. This magnificent lie pulls in hundreds of millions of dollars annually for political machines; yet George Washington warned that partisan politics is worse than useless. For over 200 years, we didn't listen to President Washington's advice. But we must stop doing what clearly doesn't work. We must have courage. Most of all, we must close our ears to lies.

Article I Section 8 of the Constitution stipulates that We The People limited our federal creature to *only 17* enumerated powers, retaining all other powers for ourselves and our sovereign States.

We can't trust politicians in State legislatures to enforce those limits. The average State legislator is as corrupt as those in Congress. From here onward, We the People must enforce the limits on our federal government through our State courts, and this includes removing corrupt State judges and seating judges who will support the Constitution; who will *"be bound thereby"*.

If AmericaAgain! grows to millions of members organized in local chapters, we will tactically mass our force, then begin to enforce the law through the courts and officers of our States. As President Andrew Jackson reminded us in his farewell address,

> In your hands is rightfully placed the sovereignty of the country, and to you everyone placed in authority is ultimately responsible. It is always in your power to see to it that the wishes of the people are carried into faithful execution...

The crimes and abdication of a century can't be excised in one election cycle, or by any number of elections. Still, the U.S. Constitution and all laws and treaties made in harmony with it are the Supreme Law, waiting for our enforcement.

Applied Christianity

Christians are optimists because we know the end of the story, that our story has no end. C.S. Lewis suggested that in the eternal scheme, one Christian is more significant than an entire civilization; thus our view of life is different from that of the atheist, hedonist, or false religionist. For us, Christ changes everything.

Mr. Obama and this corrupt Congress do not signal America's demise; only the needed spark for the Tea Party movement. And if that movement is today's Paul Revere, then AmericaAgain! is Madison on a motorcycle.

The Wounded Angel

The striking 19th century painting on the cover, *The Wounded Angel* was painted by Hugo Simberg and now hangs in the National Gallery of Finland. Boys carry a stricken angel through Elaintarha Park towards the Blind Girls' School and the Home for Cripples.

The expression of the boy in the rear embodies the bitterness in the hearts of many American children. The angel is America's institutional church – a subject requiring a book by itself[5] – with elaborate facilities, corporate structure, and programs from *Golf Tournament for Jesus, Ski-Trip for Jesus, Mediterranean Cruise for Jesus,* not to mention a fitness gym, that together virtually assure that such institutions will produce cynics and epicureans rather than season public discourse, parenting, or civil government with the counter-cultural hard teachings of Jesus Christ.

In a larger sense, the wounded angel is the original hope of the New World: to glorify Christ, a mission held hostage by religious careerists for 150 years, as Christians have sold our souls for pottage served up by the cruel Nanny State.

Simberg's painting portrays our present condition, but it need not be our future. God creates men and angels and upholds all by the power of His hand. When civilizations fall, it is *God* who chastises; when a people is renewed, it is *God* who brings new life. The chapters ahead will help you consider a few critical aspects of citizenship. I will suggest what has happened to us and why; but more constructively, I will offer my vision of a way back to the citizenship envisioned by James Madison, chief author of the Constitution. I believe that AmericaAgain! is the most tactically efficient, strategically powerful plan for self-government offered to the American people in many generations. If AmericaAgain! grows to scale it will revise our view of our responsibilities for ourselves, our children, our parents, and government *for the rest of history.*

Neither easy nor painless, it is the only practical solution being offered, and it demands less time, money, and effort than the average Tea Party calendar entails.

When I was nine years old, Ronald Reagan, among the most eloquent, astute statesmen of the 20th century, warned us that,

> If we lose freedom here, there is no place to escape to. This is the last stand on Earth. And this idea that government is beholden to the people, that it has no other source of power except to sovereign people, is still the newest and most unique idea in all the long history of man's relation to man... Whether we believe in our capacity for self-government or whether we abandon the American revolution and confess that a little intellectual elite in a far-distant capital can plan our lives for us better than we can plan them ourselves.[6]

If we will love truth and fear no man but fear God alone, we can restore a form of government and a way of life that we thought was lost forever. But first, we must grow up. We must stop believing the lies that I will now debunk *seriatim*. We have to stare government corruption square in the face, and stand against it.

But brace yourself; as you will learn in following chapters, the corruption in government is more than matched by the corruption in ourselves.

2

Lie #1:

The Constitution grants citizen rights

None calleth for justice, nor any pleadeth for truth: they trust in vanity, and speak lies; they conceive mischief, and bring forth iniquity. (Isaiah 59:4)

Knowledge will forever govern ignorance; and a people who mean to be their own governors must arm themselves with the power that knowledge gives. (James Madison)

I will offer an analogy so that you can appreciate what is happening to you; what will happen to our children if we fail to act.

When We The People created federal government, we were parents giving birth to a baby. Given man's sin nature, it wasn't long before we parents began to allow our child to get away with fibs and small sins. As it grew, it tempted groups of citizens into sharing stolen loot; soon, we allowed it to pull off ever-larger crimes. Andrew Jackson was the last president to exercise the horizontal check-and-balance duty. Love of money being the root of all evil, that is what we've had ever since: *all evil.*

A superb book by former Idaho Rep. Phil Hart[1] details how Congress brewed its fraudulent IRS scheme from 1909-1913; in our day, Congress has become so brazenly dismissive of the Constitution that if they announced that the supreme law is now dead, nothing in Washington, D.C. would need to change.

We the People were the creators of our federal government through the Constitution; we are the sovereign over it. However, generations of government-run education had its intended effect; most Americans are ignorant of civics. Even well-educated ones believe that our Constitution is positive law controlling our lives; that the U.S. Constitution, rather than God, grants our rights. ......
Believing its lies[2], we've allowed Congress to operate as a crime cartel for 150 years, spinning clever language to push its cancerous tendrils into all of life.

Most citizens today have no idea that the Constitution is our permanent law to *limit Leviathan* and to secure the rights that God grants mankind. The U.S. Constitution and all laws made pursuant to it and treaties made under the authority of the U.S. are "the supreme Law of the Land"; *every State judge is bound not only to obey it, but to enforce it.*

We The People defined the legislative branch in Article I, enumerating only 17 things we will allow federal government to do. In the Ninth and Tenth Amendments we stipulate that we retain *all other powers* for ourselves and our sovereign States. Regardless how many things politicians have gotten away with by using clever language, every time they do something not *specifically* enumerated, they are committing theft, fraud, and conspiracy to defraud.

These *crimes* usually surpass tens of millions of dollars; often billions of dollars. If anyone else attempted this, they'd be locked up immediately; but perpetrators in Congress convince groups of citizens to take part of the loot and to publicly support the crime.

It's time to say no to corruption. The federal government is limited to only those powers we *specifically* granted, and there is no statute of limitations on these high crimes. AmericaAgain! will begin to perform our citizen duties, assuring that State courts and law enforcement perform their duty to arrest high crimes, even if it's never been done before.

It has always been the citizens' duty to exercise our *vertical* check-and-balance when Congress violates the Constitution, which is the manufacturer's instructions for federal government – and We The People are the manufacturer.

Our sociopath criminal child runs taxpayers' lives, skimming their paychecks before they even see them because we've failed to learn basic civics and to do our duty as the sovereigns in our system of government. To discipline our child as Madison and Jefferson directed; to 'keep our Republic' as Franklin said, we must stop being ignorant, negligent parents, afraid of their criminal child.

Two-thirds of Americans still file tax returns, so Leviathan continues to rake in *five times* the revenues required to fund its lawful powers. All of us have neglected to take action against crime in Congress; never teamed up as sovereigns, to draft our own reform legislation. Now we resolve to stop fearing our creature; to bring it back under the rule of law *for the rest of history.*

3

Lie #2:

The Supremacy Clause means federal trumps State

*A son honoureth his father, and a servant his master…
if I be a master, where is my fear?* (Malachi 1:6a)

*For having lived long, I have experienced many instances of being obliged, by
better information or fuller consideration, to change opinions, even on important subjects, which I once thought right but found to be otherwise.*
(Ben Franklin)

For generations, federal government has grown like a cancer into
every area of life. The government we created to serve us and
our sovereign states now demands to be treated as master. Can this
perversion from a government of enumerated powers into a limitless
Leviathan *really* be construed from the Supremacy Clause? Article
VI, Clause 2 of the U.S. Constitution reads:

> This Constitution, and the Laws of the United States
> which shall be made in Pursuance thereof; and all Treaties
> made, or which shall be made, under the Authority of the

United States, shall be the supreme Law of the Land; and the Judges in every State shall be bound thereby, any Thing in the Constitution or Laws of any State to the Contrary notwithstanding.

When those words were written, the American republic was holding together tenuously. Testing the new federal government by asserting themselves, State courts occasionally ran afoul of the U.S. Constitution. In the 19th century, such incursions were most often related to slavery; the Supremacy Clause was used to defend individual rights, bringing a State law under the aegis of the U.S. Constitution. Today, things are very different.

Since the War to Enslave the States[1], federal government has increasingly violated the U.S. Constitution. With all three branches of our federal creature turned against their creators, it's the duty of *the courts of the sovereign States* to defend the supreme Law, as James Madison, the Constitution's chief author, suggests:

(T)he government created by this compact was not made the exclusive or final judge of the extent of the powers delegated to itself...that would have made its discretion, and not the Constitution, the measure of its powers; but...as in all other cases of compact...each party has an equal right to judge for itself, as well of infractions as of the mode and measure of redress.[2]

Since the federal law guild's traditional reading of the Supremacy Clause is antithetical to Madison, how can we citizens restore rule of law, when it's impossible to bring a federal case against Congress?

AmericaAgain! has a tactical answer: our chapters approach our State grand juries for criminal indictments of our *individual* U.S. senators and congressmen for violating criminal statutes *of our State*. As corrupt members of Congress plunder taxpayer accounts through the IRS and violate the Constitution with impunity, our fresh interpretation of the Supremacy Clause uses Madison's common sense with *purely intrastate* actions.

With Madison's words above in mind, we see the Supremacy Clause with unclouded eye: *"shall be the supreme Law of the Land; and the Judges in every State shall be bound thereby...".* Every State judge is bound by the Supremacy Clause not only to obey the Constitution but to *protect it* from conspirators in Congress who, in defrauding and tyrannically controlling those whom they pretend to represent, are simultaneously violating their State penal codes.

4

Lie #3:

Judicial review is only federal

He leads counselors away spoiled, and makes the judges fools.
(Job 12:17)

*Ambitious encroachments of the federal government on the
authority of the State governments would not excite the
opposition of a single State or of a few States only;
they would be signals of general alarm.*
(James Madison)

When one asserts in court that a law is unconstitutional, if the court decides to hear the case the process is called *judicial review.* Since *Marbury v Madison* in 1803, the federal law guild has always told us that judicial review is only performed by the federal courts, whether a State or federal law is involved.

That's a problem when Congress is violating the Constitution because Article III of the Constitution stipulates that the federal courts are created by, and serve at the pleasure of, Congress. The federal courts belong to Congress, in other words; after its century-long criminal orgy, we the parents are very tired of this.

We don't have to take this, according to the Constitution's primary author. In his *Virginia Resolutions* Madison said,

> The States, then, being the parties to the constitutional compact, and in their sovereign capacity, it follows of necessity that there can be no tribunal above their authority to decide...whether the compact made by them be violated; and consequently that as the parties to it, they must themselves decide...such questions as may be of sufficient magnitude to require their interposition

Unfortunately, Madison did not clarify exactly *how* our States should do this. Whenever State courts have sought to review unconstitutional federal laws, the federal law guild has called it a political question. This left State legislatures to pass *nullification* resolutions as their only remedy short of secession.

Nullification is a State's declaration that a federal law it considers unconstitutional will neither be obeyed nor honored in that State. Jefferson liked the idea; Madison was ambivalent. At this writing, nullification actions are being pasted all over the walls in many States, led by white knights with rubber swords who just happen to be running for office.

Besides being mere political theater, the other obvious problem with nullification is that every State would soon have its own version of the Constitution for the United States.

The federal law guild tells us essentially that we must just allow Leviathan to continue to review *itself*, making the People and sovereign States pay for the damage. After all, it *has* grown so much larger than its parents!

For over a century, the only solution left to the States and the People to 'review' unconstitutional actions by Congress is either another attempt at secession, or this nullification fiasco, or of course the voting booth, a poor third place. Electing a few less-corrupt ones to counter the corrupt D.C. horde is like pouring a cup of lemonade into a pitcher of raw sewage and hoping the result will be fit for the table.

AmericaAgain! is bringing a new twist to judicial review that is totally consistent with Madison: if a citizen of Texas just happens to serve in Congress and violates the Constitution in that capacity he can be indicted, tried, convicted, sentenced, and confined in a Texas State Penitentiary for crimes under the Texas Penal Code that fit his activities.

The barons did not go to King John; they demanded that he come to their tent at Runnymede in 1215 A.D. to affix his seal to *Magna Carta* – thus admitting that he was not above the law. No more caravans to D.C.; Congress is not above the law and will now be required to come home to face constituents in State Court when they violate the Supreme Law.

5

Lie #4:

Sovereign Immunity means Congress is Untouchable

When the righteous are in authority, the people rejoice: but when the wicked beareth rule, the people mourn. (Proverbs 29:2b)

Do not separate text from historical background. If you do, you will have perverted and subverted the Constitution, which can only end in a distorted, bastardized form of illegitimate government.
(James Madison)

B ecause federal judges repeat this lie so often, Americans have come to believe it without searching the Constitution or the framers' writings. Once you do so, you can see that the idea is not only illogical, but simply wicked. Article I, Section 6, Clause 2 of the U.S. Constitution reads as follows:

> They shall in all Cases, except Treason, Felony and Breach of the Peace, be privileged from Arrest during their Attendance at the Session of their respective Houses, and in going to and returning from the same; and for any Speech or Debate

in either House, they shall not be questioned in any other Place.

The legislative history behind this clause is basically that the framers drew it from Britain's parliamentary custom that assured freedom of speech while in their legislature. Author John Remington Graham offers a detailed background of the intent, tracing back to the reign of Henry VIII in English law.[1]

Reading the plain language in the clause itself, it's *absurd* to conclude that members of Congress can commit crimes without being punished for them!

The U.S. Supreme Court spoke to this issue, of politicians having supposed 'sovereign immunity':

> Counsel for the claimant…makes a very ingenious argument… (t)hat the maxim of English constitutional law, that the King can do no wrong, is one which the courts must apply to the government of the United States, and that therefore there can be no tort committed by the government. It is not easy to see how (this) proposition can have any place in our system of government…(T)he English maxim does not declare that the government, or those who administer it, can do no wrong; for it is a part of the principle itself that wrong may be done by the governing power, for which the ministry, for the time being, is held responsible; and the ministers personally, like our president, may be impeached; or, if the wrong amounts to a crime, they may be indicted and tried at law for the offense. We do not understand that either in reference to the government of the United States, or of the several states, or of any of their officers, the English maxim has an existence in this country. *Langford v. United States,* 101 U.S. 341 (1879)

Yet, I have spoken to attorneys, one of them a former judge, who when first presented with our tactical plan for the AmericaAgain!

Indictment Engine™ responded that Congress enjoys sovereign immunity and can't be prosecuted for crimes.

The clause only stipulates that members cannot be hauled away while in session or traveling to or from a session of Congress, except in cases of treason, felony, or breach of the peace. This is not a problem. These multi-trillion-dollar felons needn't worry that their sheriff from back home will seize them while they're ensconced in Congress. But they have to come home *sometime.*

6

Lie #5:

Everything is interstate commerce

Oh let the wickedness of the wicked come to an end;
but establish the just…(Psalm 7:9a)

Every government degenerates when trusted to the rulers alone;
the people themselves are its only safe depositories.
(Thomas Jefferson)

———————

No modern author has done more to awaken Americans to our duties over the Constitution than FOX News analyst, former New Jersey Judge Andrew Napolitano, some of whose books are outlined in *Suggested Reading*. Over the years, Judge Napolitano has pointed out countless examples of federal government's violating its own laws and the Constitution.

The three branches of servant government are sworn to support the Constitution, but since Lincoln's time they have employed terror tactics to coerce citizens, placing themselves above laws while placing us, their sovereigns, under those laws.

One of Congress' favorite tactics to thus pervert law is to declare things to be *interstate commerce*. Federal courts extend federal power further into our lives; areas properly overseen by State judiciaries, not federal courts, having no connection to the 17 powers that we granted to federal government. As with the Necessary and Proper and the General Welfare clauses, Congress has grown adept at this stretching exercise, and will continue in this way until We The People learn civics.

Civilization's lifeblood

As I suggested in the opening sentence of this work, truth is civilization's keystone; forfeited, it becomes its headstone. George Orwell said that "in times of universal deceit, telling the truth becomes a revolutionary act". I might add that in such times as ours, it is also a very *rare* act.

Universal deceit is exacting its price. In no part of organic society is truth more vitally absent than the justice system. Americans now have as little contact as possible with the courts. They fear judges rather than respect them because they're seen to be as corrupt as lawyers, and lawyer jokes arise as much from cynicism or disgust as from good humor.

America's judicial hierarchy

All federal courts inferior to the U.S. Supreme Court are established by Congress. Federal judges are appointed by presidents but federal courts only exist at Congress' pleasure, per Article III of the U.S. Constitution.

Try to grasp this because in most citizens' minds, the federal courts are a higher species than courts of the States. This is reversed; federal courts don't exist primarily for citizens' benefit, but for that of Congress. If you doubt me, read Article III.

In light of the Sunday night communist hijacking of the health-care system in March 2010, understand something that you will never learn in school, college, or from *Law & Order* dramas: if Congress decided to shut down the federal courts tomorrow, there would be no more federal courts inferior to the U.S. Supreme Court. Period.

Citizens could do nothing about it, for all inferior federal courts are Congress' creatures.

However, We The People have our own courts in every State, and while Congress can shut down or restrict the kinds of issues that federal courts will hear, it cannot do this to our courts in the States. For most legal issues that arise in life, our State courts and *not federal courts,* are the People's tribunal.

You do have business in federal courts if an issue arises between you or your State against another State, your State judiciary can't adjudicate actions of another State. The same holds when you have cause against your servant federal government or its operatives who commit a tort or crime against you; take it to federal court – and good luck.

Now do you see why Congress can make a horrific law or can have its own courts re-label areas of life with no connection to any enumerated power of federal government, as 'interstate commerce'; because if we're crazy enough to go there for justice, the servant of our servant will be happy to act as our master.

Public schools have superintended most citizens' education for many generations, thus civics and the U.S. Constitution are almost totally foreign information. Most citizens believe that federal courts are a higher breed of court than State courts; they think that federal court trumps State Court but the *opposite* is true.

Madison's design provides federal remedy for federal tyranny: the U.S. Supreme Court. Not created by Congress nor serving at Congress' pleasure, the U.S. Supreme Court was created by and works for We The People. As we curb our out-of-control federal servant we have two advocates, our U.S. Supreme Court and our State Courts – *both of which* trump the inferior federal courts.

Making our spoiled children behave

Obviously, federal judges won't like a new arrangement. That's a frivolous issue; we haven't liked what our federal creature has been illegally doing to us for a century but they did it anyway. Now it's the parents' turn. The difference is, we will have the Constitution on our side.

Americans regard the U.S. Supreme Court as deity, but James Madison never put much stock in that branch checking the other two. Madison certainly never ascribed to it the godlike power it enjoys in the public mind today. Larry Kramer, dean of Stanford Law School, puts our citizen duty in the clearest terms:

> The question Americans must ask themselves is whether they are comfortable handing the Constitution over to the forces of aristocracy: whether they share this lack of faith in themselves and their fellow citizens, or whether they are prepared to assume once again the full responsibilities of self-government. And make no mistake, the choice is ours to make, necessarily and unavoidably. The Constitution does not make it for us. Neither does history or tradition or law… (T)o control the Supreme Court, we must first lay claim to the Constitution ourselves. That means publicly repudiating justices who say that they, not we, possess ultimate authority to say what the Constitution means. It means publicly reprimanding politicians who insist that…we should submissively yield to whatever the Supreme Court decides. It means refusing to be deflected by arguments that constitutional law is too complex or difficult for ordinary citizens… Above all, it means insisting that the Supreme Court is our servant and not our master… The Supreme Court is not the highest authority in the land on constitutional law. We are. [1]

The Madisonian principle in Dean Kramer's words are the fuel of the AmericaAgain! Indictment Engine™. We The People have a sovereign duty over the U.S. Supreme Court, but even more of a duty to oversee, and to have our State Court indict and convict our own members of Congress when they violate the Supreme Law.

In the case of corrupt presidents, We the People have indirect power; the AmericaAgain! Declaration (Appendix C) explains that

Congress can de-fund unconstitutional executive orders and if they refuse, we can pursue them for conspiracy.

Can we really expect to transform today's den of thieves into a body of statesmen again? I believe we can, if we take seriously our duty to discipline our creature by enforcing the Constitution. Once the cycle of crime is broken in Congress, see Article I Section 3; we gave the Senate the power to try impeachments. The Senate can begin to handle corrupt presidents and federal judges in our name.

This is all pie in the sky to those who believe that America is beyond law enforcement, that we are finished. In my view, our enforcing the Constitution would be one mark of a repentant society, and very definitely worth the attempt. It is far more reasonable, more easily achieved, more peaceful, and more fitting the original design for this republic than secession, demonstrations, nullification actions, anarchy, or Libertarian pie-in-the-sky.

7

Lie #6:

General welfare means the founders were socialists

Thou shalt not steal. (Exodus 20:15)

We must not look to government to solve our problems.
Government is the problem. (Ronald Reagan)

I n the Constitution are listed the 17 powers we grant to federal government, including *"provide for the…general welfare of the United States"*. What does this mean? Surely the framers didn't have the idea of general welfare that deTocqueville paints in describing socialist France in the 1830s:

> Seek(ing) only to keep them fixed irrevocably in childhood, it likes citizens to enjoy themselves, provided that they think only of enjoying themselves. It willingly works for their hap-piness; but it wants to be the sole agent and sole arbiter of that. It provides for their security, foresees and secures their needs, facilitates their pleasures, conducts their principal affairs, directs their industry, regulates their estates, divides

their inheritances. Can it not take from them entirely the trouble of thinking, the pain of living?[1]

General welfare definitely did *not* mean today's panoply of socialist powers, regulations, fees, permits, handouts, and projects pouring out of the Washington D.C. cornucopia after being extorted through IRS terrorism.

Madison knew that if the federal government arrogated to itself any powers it wanted, our own Congress would begin to subvert the law by making 'laws' for its own corrupt uses, exactly as it has been doing since Lincoln's time:

> If Congress can employ money indefinitely to the general welfare, and are the sole and supreme judges of the general welfare...everything from the highest object of state legisla-tion down to the most minute object of police would be thrown under the power of Congress.... it would subvert the very foundations, and transmute the very nature of the limited government established by the people of America.[2]

Countless books expose the innumerable unconstitutional acts, and projects undertaken by federal government today. Tales of waste and woe in school district, local, county, state, and federal govern-ment appear in newspapers and blogs across America. For illustra-tion purposes, let's consider the U.S. Department of Energy.

In 1977, Democrat president Jimmy Carter decided that it was unacceptable for America to import 30% of our oil, so he launched a government bureaucracy to solve the problem. The new central government energy ministry had one directive: to decrease American dependence on foreign oil. Has it delivered?

Well, U.S. Department of Energy spends $25 billion per year, so it is very good at spending. With 16,000 federal bureaucrats plus 100,000 contractors on the payroll, it is superb at creating make-work careers. However, after 33 years we import 70% of our oil. As the old Soviet bureaucracies and every other socialist program, it has failed miserably. Half a trillion dollars could have remained in the private economy.

Jimmy Carter's central education ministry and every other socialist federal bureaucracy not on the Constitution's list of lawful powers, is likewise an abject failure. Now, Congress is determined that we shall all have European and Canadian-style government efficiency at our doctor's offices and hospitals beginning in 2013. Millions of us say *over our dead bodies, you criminals.*

James Madison made clear that the General Welfare clause grants no powers except as enumerated in the Constitution:

> Whenever therefore, money has been raised by the general authority and is to be applied to a particular measure, a question arises *whether the particular measure be within the enumerated authorities vested in Congress.* If it be, the money requisite for it may be applied to it; if it be not, no such application can be made.[3]

Thomas Jefferson agreed; We the People and States were very specific about the powers that we wanted our new federal servant to be able to exercise:

> [O]ur tenet ever was...that Congress has not unlimited powers to provide for the general welfare, but were to those specifically enumerated; and that, as it was never meant they should raise money for purposes which the enumeration did not place under their action...[4]

A century of failed socialist experiments demonstrates that our federal government can successfully exercise only those 17 powers enumerated in the Constitution, only when monitored. As with every socialist regime in history, every attempt by Congress to exercise illicit power has proven a colossal failure.

Banks, bars, and bordellos

I'll here pose a fittingly absurd analogy to illustrate the brazen nature and extent of Congress' crime today.

Suppose you spent years building a company that makes wooden home improvement goods. Your staff of 23 each has a job description stipulated in their contract.

After a decade without a vacation, you decide to take a four month overseas jaunt. Two months into your hiatus, you check your accounts online and find that your accounts have been drained. In a panic, you catch the first flight back home.

As you drive up to your building, this is your block but obviously not your building; the façade is transformed, now split into three storefronts – a bank, a bar, and a whorehouse.

Gingerly walking into the bank as into a nightmare, you are greeted by the bank manager. Your former band saw operator is now surrounded by leather furnishings and finishes of marble, travertine, and polished bronze. "Hey, boss!" the manager chirps; "I hope you like what I've done with the place. You had plenty of money, so I opened a bank; suits me and my friends much better than operating a band saw. Hey, you want to open an account!?"

Shaking your head in shock and hot with anger, you walk next door for a drink. "Boss, you're back!" shouts your former drill-press operator, sunken eyes twinkling, his wisp of hair combed neatly over his ivory pate. "Sit right down; you look like you can really use a cold one!"

By your second beer, you notice your former workers' new cars – Mercedes, Jaguar, Bentley, Ferrari, BMW – filling the parking lot in back. You also notice they are all wearing new Niemann-Marcus attire. "None of us liked woodworking, and you were gone, so we decided to shoot for the stars with your account balances. You snooze, you lose!"

Seeing your face redden as you rise to call the sheriff, he strikes a conciliatory tone, "Don't worry; we may be living like kings and you're not. But you're still the boss! Plus hey –if you file a timely return, you'll get a smidgen of your money back. Incidentally, we help a lot of other people; we're very benevolent! Especially the girls next door."

I know the analogy is humorous, but the programs, projects, departments, agencies, contracts, and bureaucracies that Congress devises and funds in violation of law, using money illicitly skimmed from your checks, are far *more* preposterous than this analogy. To review the truly gargantuan scope of Congress' illicit operations, see the charts at http://wallstats.com/deathandtaxes, and keep a copy of Article I, Section 8 of the Constitution at hand.

General Welfare is anything they can think of to do with the money skimmed from your checks. Those trillions are coming in one way or the other, and as every bureaucrat knows: you either spend it all, or you'll get less next time. As Ronald Reagan loved to say, we get the government we pay for.

So. With most Taxpayers on vacation from their senses, and never having even seen a copy of the Tax Code but still letting Congress skim their paychecks, who is actually to blame for the fact that our employees are shooting for the stars, *boss?*

8

Lie #7:

Voting is citizens' only remedy for corruption

The way of the wicked is as darkness: they know not at what they stumble. (Proverbs 4:19)

An election is coming! Universal peace is declared, and the foxes have a sincere interest in prolonging the lives of the poultry.
(T.S. Eliot)

Political party operatives and the media suggest that a citizen's most patriotic duty is to cast a vote once every couple of years. Then it's best that voters go back to sleep, and allow the professionals to handle government. Since most voters are happy to oblige – and 43% of eligible citizens haven't voted in the past half-dozen elections – perhaps a bit of armchair sociology might clarify the game.

You may be familiar with the diagrams in butcher shops, depicting various cuts of beef mapped out on the carcass. *Beef* is cow meat and *veal* is part of a calf (don't mistake my direction; I love meat) so semantics here is a craft, not art. Certain words help drive people to certain actions.

A predator succeeds as long as he knows that once you're grouped, you'll move with the group, invariably. Since the rise of corporations in the 1950s, this principle has accomplished great things on Madison Avenue and Wall Street. It means dinner. And drinks. Chartered jets, even.

What does all this have to do with voting? Rather a lot, actually. Though it only began to influence Americans with the rise of fascism (the state and corporations allied to plunder a population) this mapping out and naming targets has been a predator's staple in senescent cultures since Greece and Rome.

Each predator group develops its own labels to describe the target masses, depending on a particular predator's use for them; basically, what you learn in marketing courses. The trick is for the masses not to get a clue until it's too late in the game; i.e., after the polls close.

You're prey and predators aren't, and it's not just a matter of brawn and sharp teeth. Predators use good labels to map the herd. In American cities over a certain size, prey-mapping terms have been instilled in citizens by the advertising and media industries for three generations.

The chart looks like this: to retailers, you're a *consumer*. If you work for a large corporation you're a human resource, a digit in a workforce; a *worker*. And to that magnificent alliance of symbiotic predators and carrion-eaters in Congress' IRS scheme, now in its third generation, you are a *taxpayer*.

If you live and move and have your being as part of a mass market, the predator's life is one big party; fish in a barrel. His job is to make feints, threats, or in some cases, promises. Any promise will do; when he fails to keep them later on, the flock has moved on to the next campaign, sales event, meaningless promotion, or 'tax season'.

Congress and State legislatures are infested with *sincere politicians* (a classic oxymoron) because as we will describe shortly, there is simply too much money in politics today. The statesman is loath to enter that atmosphere, leaving Congress to the huckster with the telegenic smile and nice hair, who will parse the demographic groups like a beef carcass, attracting each one with bait suiting that market segment: immigration, taxes, war and peace, jobs, you name it; any promise will do.

Here's the pitch: "Stay with the herd; that's your safety! Stay close to your co-worker, neighbor, co-consumer, co-voter and your duty is clear. And me? Why, I must sing!"

> *Whoopee ti yi yo, git along ye little dogies,*
> *It's your misfortune and none of my own;*
> *Whoopee ti yi yo, git along ye little dogies,*
> *You know that Wyomin' will be your new home.* [1]

9

Lie #8:

The GOP is conservative

As a cage is full of birds, so are their houses full of deceit;
therefore they are become great, and waxen rich.
(Jeremiah 5:27)

Half a truth is often a great lie. (Benjamin Franklin)

Richard Weaver's book *Ideas Have Consequences* asserted that our culture ran onto the rocks long ago, and Otto Scott's book *The Great Christian Revolution* traces our civilization to its roots. Both books suggest that American decline certainly did not begin when *Leave it To Beaver* went off the air.

To understand why the GOP will not restore limited government or rule of law, we will consider a moral watershed that came to America seven generations after the first English colony here, at the same time that the GOP was hatched.

Let me here concede the obvious: the Democrat party is equally destructive, so my point is that George Washington was right, and partisanship generally is a moral black hole.

America's Christian roots

The first book used in American collective education was the Bible. For over two centuries, and until the 1840s, the Bible and *New England Primer* comprised America's curriculum, then were joined by Noah Webster's *Grammatical Institute of the English Language,* commonly called the Blue Back Speller.

Amidst heavy early immigration from Germany (Franklin worried that they might fail to assimilate) the growing republic remained staunchly Christian. These three core texts taught generations to read, spell, and pronounce English.

These texts were Christian; children also learned spelling, grammar, vocabulary and penmanship via *copybook* – rote copying from a book, usually the King James or Geneva Bible.

Prior to Lincoln's generation, American children received limited formal education. Some families sent their children to dame schools; commonly a one-room place offering reading, writing, and ciphering lessons for a small fee. Wealthy families taught their children at home or hired tutors who trained them in the classics, languages, art, mathematics, and music.

At any rate, American education was consciously Christian from our colonial period until Lincoln's generation.

The gospel according to Karl

Government schools are an idea as old as ancient Greece, but in America, they were the brainchild of Karl Marx; the tenth point in his 1847 *Communist Manifesto,* which came to be the blueprint for transforming American life over 150 years:

1) abolish private property
2) institute a heavy progressive income tax
3) abolish all right of inheritance (corollary to #1)
4) confiscate property of emigrants and resisters (if they resist or leave the country, gov't takes their property)

5) government runs credit and banking
6) government runs communication and transportation
7) government runs industry
8) render all labor equal and create industrial armies
9) eliminate the urban/rural divide (nowhere to run)
10) government schools combine education and industry

A strategic mind will appreciate that points 2 and 10 are the critical ones. If a bureaucrat can program children, then tax them when they are old enough to work, one can do anything in government and will get very little citizen resistance. Most citizens are oblivious to American socialism, thus the government schools have achieved their *true* intended mission.

By the time Congress began its 97-year-long financial crime in 1913, government schools and liberal churches were well-established in urban areas, providing a steady stream of recruits for the military, corporations, and bureaucracy. Karl Marx's dream was now a malignant cancer in America's fiber. Wilson, FDR, LBJ, Carter, Clinton, two Bushes, Obama and the 111th Congress have erased all traces of Marx's name and the label 'socialism', which does not fit anyway because with the corporations joined in the plunder, America is not socialist but more closely aligned to classical fascism that all began in Lincoln's generation.

The Old Dark in story and rhyme

The dark mind of European humanism, ironically called Enlightenment, was an *avant garde* view of God, man, and the universe. Actually the ancient paganism of Europe, exported by the British neo-pagans and the Teutonic romantics and intellectuals of Lincoln's generation. Having dyed the cultural fabric of Europe blood red, the cultural toxin now lapped at America's shores via literature, economics, and ethics as was now taught in the public schools. Billed as a means to inculcate common American culture to waves of immigrants, to Calvinists the unspoken sub-theme of government schools was that they were an antidote to Roman Catholic schools.

The spiritual retrogression began in Lincoln's generation, also the generation of Marx and of Charles Darwin, whose *Origin of Species* appeared in 1859, and of humanists and neopagans William Blake, Percy Shelley, Emily Dickinson, Walt Whitman, Ralph Waldo Emerson, Nathaniel Hawthorne, Herman Melville, Mark Twain, James Joyce, D.H. Lawrence, Matthew Arnold, William Butler Yeats, and others.

In his book *Dismissing God,* Bruce Lockerbie exposes and analyzes these mainstays of public school literature for over a century. Other books in *Suggested Reading* expose the fascist ideology and economics that combined in Lincoln's era to make full-strength poison for all Americans.

The year after Lincoln's war ended, the transatlantic cable was laid, solidifying the belief that man was the master of his own fate. The generation of agnostic writers after the Lincoln era included such public school curriculum heroes as F. Scott Fitzgerald, William Henley, and Ernest Hemingway.

The final stanzas of Henley's best-known poem *Invictus,* so commonly recited in schools, announces man's invincibility:

> *Out of the night that covers me,*
> *Black as the pit from pole to pole,*
> *I thank whatever gods may be*
> *For my unconquerable soul*
> *…*
> *It matters not how strait the gate,*
> *How charged with punishments the scroll,*
> *I am the master of my fate:*
> *I am the captain of my soul.*

Lockerbie's book exposes the depth and breadth of cultural reprogramming that engaged the public schools for generations after Lincoln's. The founding norms and nobility that had stood for seven generations before Dishonest Abe came to power, were crushed along with the Constitution in Lincoln's war.

Lincoln's 'shock and awe' campaign

Perhaps the single most breathtaking lie taught to every American government-school student is that Abraham Lincoln was a great president. Lincoln was the *worst* American president; a fact borne out by the heavily-documented texts by Thomas DiLorenzo, Greg Durand, and Jeff Hummel listed in *Suggested Reading*. My purpose is to expose the linkage between the birth of the GOP and Lincoln's 'shock and awe' war that it is estimated killed over 650,000 Americans and destroyed 70% of total assessed property in the South. As Andrew Napolitano puts it:

> Lincoln replaced a voluntary association of states with a strong centralized government. The president and his party (the GOP) easily lifted the floodgates to the modern thuggish style of ruling that the U.S. government now employs.[1]

From the mid-19th century and for a century after, the foundation of America's unique Christian society was dismantled and hauled out of sight. I certainly don't support the idea of theocracy, but clearly, atheist rule has proven far worse for America... More to the point, from the middle of last century until today, government school students have been kept ignorant of our unique, precious form of government, instead being fed a hodgepodge of politically-correct, worthless 'social studies'.

Can it be any wonder that citizens are unequipped to even consider, much less to act upon, the idea of constitutional self-determination and rule of law?

Marx in a stovepipe hat

With this background in mind, a few facts about Lincoln before I discuss his political party.

First, Lincoln was profoundly ungodly, but had the politician's gift of pious oratory and composition.[2] Secondly, as has been common of many successful occupants of the White House, Lincoln had failed at virtually everything he had tried before and thus made an ideal puppet for mercantilists.

Thirdly, the average public school graduate does not know that Karl Marx was an avid supporter of Lincoln, or that many of Lincoln's generals were avowed Marxists. These facts may be corroborated in the books listed in *Suggested Reading* or you can dig up a great deal with a simple internet search.

The fact is, the state cheated you in your education. In order to recover America's Constitution, limited government, sound currency, and liberty, citizens must know the truth about the real purpose of The War to Enslave the States.

The Republican party as Robert E. Lee saw it

In correspondence with Lord Acton just months after the end of the war, Robert E. Lee of Virginia, the greatest general in American history, explains the part played by the GOP in causing the war. Note the italicized sections; they are my italics. First, Lord Acton's note to General Lee, then General Lee's December response:

Bologna
04 November 1866

Sir,
...

Without presuming to decide the purely legal question, on which it seems evident to me from Madison's and Hamilton's papers that the

Fathers of the Constitution were not agreed, I saw in State Rights the only availing check upon the absolutism of the sovereign will, and secession filled me with hope, not as the destruction but as the redemption of Democracy.

... I believed that the example of that great Reform would have blessed all the races of mankind by establishing true freedom purged of the native dangers and disorders of Republics. Therefore I deemed that you were fighting the battles of our liberty, our progress, and our civilization; and I mourn for the stake which was lost at Richmond more deeply than I rejoice over that which was saved at Waterloo.
...
I remain, with sentiments stronger than respect, Sir,

Your faithful servant
John Dalberg Acton

Lexington, Vir.,
15 Dec. 1866

Sir,
...
Amid the conflicting statements and sentiments in both countries, it will be no easy task to discover the truth, or to relieve it from the mass of prejudice and passion, with which it has been covered by party spirit. I am conscious the compliment conveyed in your request for my opinion as to the light in which American politics should be viewed, and had I the ability, I have not the time to enter upon a discussion, which was commenced by the founders of the Constitution and has been continued to the present day.

I can only say that while I have considered the preservation of the constitutional power of the General Government to be the foundation of our peace and safety at home and abroad, *I yet believe that the maintenance of the rights and authority reserved to the states and to the people, not only essential to the adjustment and balance of the general system, but the safeguard to the continuance of a free government. I consider it as the chief source of stability to our political system, whereas the consolidation of the states into one vast republic, sure to be aggressive abroad and despotic at home, will be the certain precursor of that ruin which has overwhelmed all those that have preceded it.*

I need not refer one so well acquainted as you are with American history, to the State papers of Washington and Jefferson, the representatives of the federal and democratic parties, denouncing consolidation and centralization of power, as tending to the subversion of State Governments, and to despotism.
...

The South has contended only for the supremacy of the Constitution, and the just administration of the laws made in pursuance to it. Virginia to the last made great efforts to save the union, and urged harmony and compromise. Senator Douglass, in his remarks upon the compromise bill recommended by the committee of thirteen in 1861, stated that every member from the South, including Messrs. Toombs and Davis, expressed their willingness to accept the proposition of Senator Crittenden from Kentucky, as a final settlement of the controversy, *if sustained by the republican party, and that the only difficulty in the way of an amicable adjustment was with the republican party.*

Who then is responsible for the war? Although the South would have preferred any honorable compromise to the fratricidal war which has taken place, she now *accepts in good faith its constitutional results, and receives without reserve the amendment which has already been made to the Constitution for the extinction of slavery. That is an event that has been long sought, though in a different way,* and by none has it been more earnestly desired than by citizens of Virginia. In other respects I trust that the Constitution may undergo no change, but that it may be handed down to succeeding generations in the form we received it from our forefathers.

...

With sentiments of great respect,
I remain your obt. servant,
R.E. Lee

Mercantilists' divide-and-conquer tactic

From the beginning, the GOP marched under the banner of Alexander Hamilton, his protégé Henry Clay, and their *American System* which had four goals: a central Bank of the U.S., massive public works projects, high tariffs, and high public land prices. America's powerful men could not achieve these goals unless they first neutralized public opposition.

America's *real* War on Terror began at Fort Sumter in 1861; the mercantilists' opening gambit for divide-and-conquer was Lincoln's war. Slavery provided a perfect distraction for brilliant billionaires who buy, sell, and trade presidents and members of Congress as children trade baseball cards. Anyone could see that the Ft. Sumter hoax made no sense, and Seward and others in Lincoln's cabinet were clearly against war, as were many in the North.

As DiLorenzo states, 13 governments had already abolished slavery without resort to war: Argentina (1813), Colombia (1814), Chile (1823), Central America (1824), Mexico (1829), Bolivia (1831), British colonies (1840), Uruguay (1842), French colonies (1848), Ecuador (1851), Peru (1854) and Venezuela (1854).

Thus I reiterate the real purpose behind the War to Enslave the States: *divide the republic into equal, offsetting halves.* If the People are turned against one another in equal armies, this means the owners of the house are kept fighting in the front yard forever, while the shrewd thieves steal the entire contents of the house, right out the back door, at their leisure.

We will discuss the two sides of the financial crime in the next two chapters; here I only seek to illustrate the tactical part played by political parties in the largest crime in history.

Divide-and-conquer is brilliant. It neutralizes the citizens by turning them against one another, leaving no time to think, to consider what is afoot. It's also much less costly and more efficient to buy and maintain one set of puppets (Congress and the White House) than to have to purchase and maintain 50 sets of legislators and governors.

Once Lincoln's federal troops had instilled shock-and-awe into the insurgent States North and South, Washington D.C. was the new master over Americans of every color, the war's real purpose.

When the war ended, North v. South was no longer a feasible basis for divide-and-conquer but the recent collapse of the Whig party allowed the mercantilists to launch the GOP, to spark a donkey v. elephant war that has continued ever since.

The pendulum of power is allowed to swing in Congress and the White House with elections, to give clueless 'voters' on both teams a glimpse of hope for their side. Party careerists and media give the perennial pep talk, "Any year now, our party platform will put a chicken in every pot, and we reclaim America! Keep up the fight against that damned opposition! Support your candidate now!" Billionaires enjoy free reign in Washington D.C. and millions of pay-rolls as 'voters' remain oblivious, trudging to the polls, planting yard signs and paying for useless money bombs.

Perennial war, an imperial industry

Besides the divide-and-conquer tactic for pillaging one's own citizens, war has always been a hugely profitable industry in its own right, and a diversion for domestic plunder. Regardless how tenuous or shaky the facts, *"the threat demands a response!"* became an effective rallying cry since Fort Sumter.

The pattern of every American war after our War for Independence has been: first, cause or allow a perceived threat to the nation; next, call forth a national military to meet the crisis; finally, place young and old, men and women under command of central government with powers never authorized by the framers of the Constitution.

Teddy Roosevelt, Woodrow Wilson, FDR, Bill Clinton and G.W. Bush and their congresses were masters of this ploy, but Obama and the 111th are learning fast; if we don't act soon, they may impose unalloyed Marxism on the 50 States at last.

Remember: the idea is divide and conquer; keep the sovereign People and States confused, busy, terrorized, and feeling powerless despite the Constitution's clear language, and then skim their checks as they argue with one another. The assault did not begin with Wilson or FDR, but with Lincoln's shock-and-awe campaign that transformed the American psyche. Fear of federal troops was designed to make citizens forget our Constitution; every war since that one has seared the new creature-creator order more deeply into the citizen consciousness. As with every other government in history, lies are now true.

Dan Rather labeled them the Greatest Generation, but my parents' generation was the most gullible: "My government, right or wrong! If my government says it, it must be true!"

Stuck on stupid: a century-long pattern

The 'unexplained' sinking of the U.S.S. Maine allowed federal forces to engage in the Spanish-American War; then the U.S. military invaded and *has kept effective possession of:* Hawaii, the Philippines, Guam, Puerto Rico, the U.S. Virgin Islands, the Marshall Islands, Wake Island, Samoa, Jarvis Island, Micronesia, Northern Mariana Islands, Palau, and now it is working hard on two much tougher imperial outposts: Afghanistan and Iraq.

In other lands, U.S. federal troops did not remain because no corporate assets existed to defend with free mercenaries: Korea, Vietnam, Haiti, Bosnia, etc. But the pattern is clear: the sinking of the U.S.S. Maine was the common theme in the sinking of the U.S.S. Lusitania (the U.S. government's entry into WWI), the attack on Pearl Harbor (entry into WWII), the supposed attack on the U.S.S. Maddox in the Gulf of Tonkin (entry into the Vietnam war), the unexplained anomalies in the 911 attacks, and various other skirmishes that have generated *hundreds of billions of dollars* in military sector revenues, and continue to do so today.

As a side benefit that garners citizen prayers and support, these actions produce careers for otherwise unemployable youth. As English, French, Dutch, Portuguese, and Spanish governments had done for centuries, America's new imperial power deploys clueless but patriotic youth overseas, to claim and defend corporate asset claims at no cost to corporations.

Grand Old Party, indeed

At the heart of all this blood and money one finds the GOP more deeply involved than the Democrat party; Lincoln was its earliest poster-boy, John McCain its latest. Whatever else may be said about them, thank God for the Tea Party movement and Glenn Beck for helping conservatives to realize that the GOP is anything but constitutionalist.

Too many GOP acolytes have exchanged the blessed assurance of their grandparents, "my God will make it right", for a new humanist faith that "my GOP will make it right".

For over 150 years, Congress has been driven by those who control politicians from behind the scenes; men whose only allegiance is to their bank accounts. They first assured that the federal government became master over its sovereign creators here at home. Having done that, they could then enslave the people of any small, resource-rich state anywhere on earth.

In his book *Overthrow: America's century of regime change from Hawaii to Iraq*, Stephen Kinzer asserts that our government's colonial acquisitions from 1893-2010 have been a mess. But Mr. Kinzer must understand that for those who run Congress from behind the scenes, the mess has been worthwhile. Each overthrow has resulted in natural resources, pipeline routes, oilfields, airfields, radar and communication sites, nuclear testing sites, and more. Defying the founders' intentions about national defense, this is all made possible by money skimmed from taxpayer paychecks.

Domestic enemies transformed America into everything the founders despised, with Congress their lapdog in atrocities. Yes, our child is a pathological, murderous criminal and We The People, the parents, must begin the discipline that we've held back for too long. The GOP is no part of the solution; *it is part of the problem.*

The Christian Left (American Socialist Party) introduced socialism in America in the 19th century, while the Christian Right has supported the very military industrial complex about which President Eisenhower warned us in 1961.

I will not ascribe evil intent to my fellow Christians if once they know the truth, they cut this foolishness with the GOP.

The waylaid Ron Paul Revolution

A principled statesman, Ron Paul attempted the impossible: first mounting repeated third party challenges, then coalescing three extremely unlikely fringe groups to support a GOP candidate.

Learning after many years as a Libertarian that a third party will never be allowed in the game by the donkey and elephant machine, Ron Paul believed he had discovered a winning coalition made of conservative Christians and three fringe groups, all of whom supported certain of Ron Paul's ideas. I believe he read the support correctly with the Christians, not with the others.

The fringe groups are Libertarians, anarchists, and atheists. Ron Paul deeply believes in the U.S. Constitution but assumes that it will never be enforced. The fringe groups do not believe in the Constitution; in fact, do not believe in government. Because he speaks so harshly against the government's *conduct*, these fools assume that he is against government's *existence*. They feel that their hour has come, for revolution, armed insurrection, secession, and anarchy. Self-delusion heaped upon lunacy, with poor Dr. Paul as their unwilling bell-cow.

Remember, voting is only a small part of our citizen duty; We The People now play divide-and-conquer. Instead of letting our opponent split us into two warring factions, we divide Congress; bring them home to 535 courts of our sovereign States. In Chapter 12 you will see details of the AmericaAgain! mechanism; peacefully, from our home and office computers, we assemble a massive citizen force and *leave partisan politics forever.*

Goodbye, GOP; instead, we begin to enforce the Constitution as Madison and Jefferson said we must. We The People control Congress right from our millions of homes, as is our citizen duty. We stay in the fight for the rest of history. The Internet makes it simple, painless, powerful, and inevitable.

10

Lie #9:

Congress can grant a counterfeiting concession

*For the love of money is the root of all evil, which while some
coveted after, they have erred from the faith, and
pierced themselves through with many sorrows.*
(I Timothy 6:10)

*Before the names of just and unjust can have place,
there must be some coercive power.*
(Thomas Hobbes)

As we saw in Chapter 2, the Supreme Court in its *Olmstead*
ruling opined that government "teaches the whole people by
its example. Crime is contagious. If the government becomes a lawbreaker, it breeds contempt for law."

As federal courts often do, the court here had the process back-
wards. We The People first allow our government to lie, steal, and
cheat to such an extent that the bad example begins to go both ways.
It may be that our criminal child now teaches its parents, but let us
remember that we *are* its parents.

There is no higher law in America than the Constitution, and the very existence of the Federal Reserve violates that law; millions of Americans know it. Thus, millions of children break the rules in school; then as adults, coached by 'financial peace' gurus selling books and programs, millions of couples walk away from huge credit card balances yet enjoy the items purchased with the cards. Theft seems acceptable not only because the winsome radio host condones it, but because everyone does it: credit card-issuing banks, Congress, and the Federal Reserve. Even the dollar is just paper; it's all a game.

Attributing moral turpitude in modern society is quite a task; where does one begin to draw the shores of a virtual *ocean* of remorseless immorality? Can truth be known? The financial industry includes so many bottom-feeders: bankers, currency traders, mortgage companies, derivatives swappers, short sellers and day traders who know nothing, and care even less, about the individuals, cultures, and companies whose lifeblood they trade in every day. Their careers consist of reveling in a margin, living on the flip and the trade; skimming a few basis points here and there plus a fee – soon, one is seriously rich.

Far from the Protestant work ethic that made America what we once were, we not only join Europe but now teach the world to play the massive casino. Because the work is so effortless and the profits so massive, government regulation becomes an impossible task, at least without independent citizen oversight, which is nonexistent today.

Watching the watchers

Citizens simply have not known how to oversee their government. Voters believe they can trust electoral politics, or can shift our oversight duty to easily-bought regulatory bodies. But the remedy to criminal government is not another layer of regulation, but decentralized oversight by millions of citizens.

When crime is in control, central bureaucracy is the least effective means to arrest it. In Mexico, for instance, the law enforcement and military officials who deal with drug cartels have learned that a sufficient number of ruthless killings and oceans of cash limit the regulator's choices to three: leave them alone, join them, or die.

As sovereigns responsible for law enforcement in America, citizens believe ourselves to be in the same moral dilemma: Wall Street, Main Street, and Capitol Hill send lessons in criminality from creators to creature and back again in daily, mutually-reinforcing retrogression. Have we reached Mexico's point of no return, of *leave them alone, join them, or die?*

Every American a swindler

The temptation to lie, steal, and cheat has grown with each generation. The prime teacher is Congress via its IRS scheme; another example is its bailout of banksters and government-backed mortgage securities giants Fannie Mae and Freddie Mac, government-sponsored enterprises launched during the FDR and Nixon administrations.

The latest round in the spiral of financial immorality began in 2007 as Congress used taxpayer funds to bail out billionaire banks. The public lesson was clear: *there are no rules.*

Today, millions of Americans live in their homes for months or years without making mortgage payments; 'strategic default' is a tactic much like the house-flipping that took place for years on the two coasts. Homebuyers bought, held, and sold residential real estate with no intention of making a home, but purely for the flip, in some cases pocketing six figures. The result: absurd prices, and immoral lessons learned.

Many couples using the strategic default tactic are telling of the Hawaii vacation or new car(s) bought with what they are 'saving' by not making mortgage payments while continuing to live in the house until the lender forecloses, if ever.

This all makes sense in the world that Washington D.C. created over the past century. Crime *does* pay; Congress does as it pleases. Judges 17:6 puts it, "there was no king in Israel, and each man did what was right in his own eyes."

Local taxing authorities play a more immoral, ruthless game in states with property taxes. A man's home is the state's castle; taxing entities auction off elderly couples' homes when they are unable to finance the neighbor children's education, splitting the plunder with their collections attorneys.

We The People can end widespread feudal plunder only if we cease acting as serfs, use tactical wisdom, and demand ethics and accountability. When Congress, your school board, or a 'financial peace' guru sends the opposite message, know that *thou shalt not steal* is the commandment. We must begin to enforce it, and must begin to publicly frown on theft.

Gold is money, keystrokes are not

Despite these heinous acts, the most devastating financial crime has been committed by corrupt congresses and bankers over the past 175 years in America. As Michael Gruber said, "villains are just there, like rust – dull and almost chemical in the stupid simplicity of their greed or pride". Henry Clay lost every political battle he ever fought, yet there are three banks on every block in America's cities and the Federal Reserve cartel is more powerful than ever. The dangers that presidents Thomas Jefferson and Andrew Jackson warned us about now have America bloodied, bruised, and on her knees.

Banks produce what they call 'money' out of thin air and keystrokes. AmericaAgain! will draft and push passage of the long-overdue *Lawful American Currency and Banking Act* because as Thomas Jefferson and Andrew Jackson said, either the Constitution will be enforced or bankers will destroy the American People and our U.S. Dollar. Only Congress has power to coin our money and regulate its value; that is its *duty* per the Supreme Law. Instead, Congress first conspired in 1913 to grant a counterfeiting concession to the Federal Reserve, a private bank cartel. Congress has acquiesced in or maintained that conspiracy for 97 years, and that crime *must end*.

Let us cut the puppeteer strings

To grasp the staggering extent of the coming depression, see the video at www.inflation.us/videos. As that video attests, for 150 years, villains have pulled yapping puppies on a leash: senator, congressman, president. These mercantilists are respected because they employ many Americans; but to save this republic, we few millions must cut the strings by which these brutes control Congress. If we number in the millions and do not relent, we can do it. Indeed, after a century of financial fraud, we *must*.

Yes, the bankers will despise us and it will rock the financial world; but if God grants this boon to the American people, our gold-backed dollar will be the world standard currency again for generations, demonstrating that in His mercy, God has not yet finished with the American People.

11

Lie #10:

Congress can run a domestic terror operation

If you see the oppression of the poor, and violent perverting
of justice and righteousness in a place, marvel not: for
that official is watched by a higher one...
(Ecclesiastes 5:8a)

A family with the wrong members in control; that, perhaps, is
as near as one can come to describing England in a phrase.
(George Orwell)

———————

Anyone familiar with organized crime will agree that the problem with Washington D.C. is as with drug cartels; too much money. Congress is pulling in five times the revenues needed to fund its lawful powers; thus, while many groups are 'helped' by this criminal activity, the legal reality remains.

This will be the most unpopular chapter of the book, but your cowardice threatens my grandchildren's liberty; it renders pointless the blood of past patriots, thus I must press you to look at your captors by the light of day. The price of moral cowardice in one generation is chains for the next.

Your own D.C. al-Qaeda

Congress would never admit that it operates a terrorist organization, but ask any taxpayer if he fears his government, and the IRS will invariably be mentioned.

The Internal Revenue Service is only Congress' bag man; it is not the boogeyman, nor is it a judicial or law-enforcement entity; it is administrative. Congress is the kingpin of the operation. *Please understand this; it is critical.*

Next, please realize the corrupting power of $3.8 trillion pouring in every year; that's approximately *$7.2 billion* under the control of each member of Congress. [1] Yet it shrewdly distances itself from the check-skimming operations in American businesses and from the terrorist collection tactics used against taxpayers.

Congress depicts IRS as a black-hooded executioner, and because the agency is under the executive branch aegis, taxpayers do not understand that Congress runs the show.

Then, Congress forces businesses to skim workers' checks; thus business owners also wear black hats. Vivien Kellems made this clear in her 1952 book *Toil, Taxes, and Trouble* but few citizens listened, and withholding was rammed through – as were Medicare, Social Security, TARP, Fannie Mae, Freddie Mac, the socialist seizure of GM, payoffs to Wall Street, and the recent socialist hijacking of the healthcare industry.

Having created its two bad cops – a ruthless IRS drone in a brown suit, and your employer's HR manager – members of Congress then painted themselves as humble public servants, defending you every day from their D.C. offices. Even con artist Bernie Madoff did not display such *chutzpah.* The largest financial scam in history is being run by those who are charged with making our laws! Their mendacity matches their audacity.

It's no wonder that Congress' approval rating has hovered around 10% for years; but they are not concerned with ratings, nor would you be if you had an ATM machine producing $7.2 billion for your control each year.

This outrage is now causing public backlash in the streets, but as I explain in the next chapter and Appendix D, there is a wide array of careerists who run interference for the system; industries that you never realized were celebrating tax season.

But we are *all* pirates now

One might contend that there exists a moral equivalency between the plunder committed daily in the halls of Congress and the plunder committed daily in the Gulf of Aden off the African coast. I do not hold that view.

If you were to interview the average villager at home base when Somalian pirates bring home a $2 million ransom, you would hear that everyone in the village is happy, the ship is steaming on its way again, the target had insurance, and what's not to like? Indeed, 'the system' works.

On most days, the pirate prepares his meager lunch, takes up his plastic bucket and AK-47, climbs aboard his fiberglass panga, and plies the African coast. Lord Nelson in blackface.

Hassan would explain that "the predatory life is still a life, you know. Must not the baby lion and hyena eat, even as the baby gazelle? Indeed, pirates have wives and children as you do, and so in place of law it is only this: will I outrun my prey, outsmart him, or overpower him?"

There is no law in Somalia; instead, there is calculation. "The boat needs gasoline. My family is hungry, so I must have a good week. If Mahmud and I refuse to go today, someone else will go. The AIS on mother ship shows an Italian flagged freighter bearing for the attack point at only 15 knots; such an easy target! *This will be a good week, I think.*"

As a lion with gazelles, as a drug cartel with the frightened Mexican people. As Congress with the American taxpayer, the pirate in an Armani suit goes to work each day, his allegiance to power and his dull, chemical certainty that a predator's work feeds many mouths.

This is 'the system'; it has produced excellent returns for corruption and for predatory traditions, ever since Congress seized its first freighter via the 16th Amendment many years ago. Within a generation, it pushed its prey into two European wars and coerced America's employers to launch the boats, make the raids, and take hostages while it watched from the beach. Now there are *many* on the beach; the system is an industry that celebrates Tax Season in the same way that retailers celebrate Christmas Season.

So. Now you see how it is with pirates. When Pelosi, Reid, Frank, et al appear on the screen, just turn off the sound and read the lips: *"This will be a good week, I think."*

Tax Honesty: The empire strikes back

If you still keep records and file forms with the IRS, and allow it or your 'employer' to skim your paychecks, you are a *Taxpayer*. Many taxable events and activities are listed in the Tax Code; if your domicile or activities fit any of those, then per 26 USC 7701(a)14, you are a *Taxpayer* by operation of law. Otherwise, you accept the title and burden of 'taxpayer': a) by ignorance, b) by employer coercion, or c) as a victim of state-sponsored terrorism. This exhausts all possibilities.

Many Americans no longer wink at crime or cringe at boogeymen; as of 2005 there were an estimated 67 million non-filers. In my case, after two years of studying Congress' IRS scam, I became a Nontaxpayer 11 years ago; for six years, I have hosted the *Tax Honesty Primer* website, see Appendix D.

Compare the huge federal government today to the mere 17 powers we granted federal government in the Constitution. Bloated government is a direct result of Congress having IRS skim America's paychecks; thus the most effective way to reduce government is to cut its funding a household at a time.

Millions more must learn the truth about Congress' 1909-1913 scam that has enslaved taxpayers ever since.[2] They must join us in lawfully cutting back federal revenues to only that which is required to fund enumerated federal powers.

Tipping the tea kettle

As the original Boston Tea Party, today's Tea Party is a signal flare that the People are making an historic move. In his bestselling book *Tipping Point,* Malcolm Gladwell defines an information-age phenomenon that resembles the propagation curve of epidemics. At a tipping point, circumstances combine to suddenly ramp an idea logarithmically; it 'goes viral'.

In the next chapter I will describe AmericaAgain! and expose the array of predators and parasites who will be forced to leave careers in the system if this is indeed history's tipping point for American self-government.

12

Madison on a motorcycle: AmericaAgain!

*But whoso looketh into the perfect law of liberty, and continueth
therein, he being not a forgetful hearer but a doer of
the work, this man shall be blessed in his deed.*
(James 1:25)

*Who are the best keepers of the People's liberties? The People themselves.
The sacred trust can be nowhere so safe as in the hands
most interested in preserving it.*
(James Madison)

Washington, D.C. corruption is staggering. Consider just one major case, the multi-trillion-dollar counterfeiting concession that Congress grants to the Federal Reserve. Per the Constitution, every member of Congress since 1913 has committed high crimes every day in office, conspiring or acquiescing in racketeering.

Evil exists; we are neither perfectionists nor utopians. Yet we have a duty to stand up to criminal government. We must re-learn how to grapple with Madison's magnificent Constitution. Farmers once discussed it as readily as we now discuss sports.

As sovereigns, we have failed to react to corruption because we lack the time to even think; led by the nose with bread and circuses "around the world in 90 seconds" through a whirl and din of irrelevant action having nothing to do with us, and about which we can do nothing. This information overload is designed to keep us busy in a cubicle, world without end, cheering for our team as unthinking middle-schoolers at a pep rally. This tactic feeds many more parasites and predators than you've ever realized.

Down the rabbit hole

Our government is deeply corrupt. We get this, but we still miss the causes of America's ongoing collapse. Grasping the full breadth of our predator-and-parasite sector requires that we ask the ancient Roman prosecutor's question, *cui bono?* Who benefits? In the jargon of the investigative journalists, follow the money.

Before it was co-opted by the GOP, the Tea Party movement discovered a piece of the puzzle: America's political pep rally is run by two equally corrupt party machines. As we discussed in earlier chapters, the two equal-and-opposite parties have served the mercantilists and party machines beautifully for generations.

But the Tea Party movement has not descended deep enough, to the full cast of operatives that wittingly or not, keep Americans from seeing the challenge clearly. I am not referring to the CFR, UN, or black helicopters; I mean your neighbor, your relative, your co-worker, or perhaps even you.

The February 7, 2009 cover story of Newsweek magazine was entitled "We Are All Socialists Now"; its subtitle claiming that "… our economy already resembles a European one. As boomers age and spending grows, we will become even more French."

Like hell we will. For the first 300 years since colonization, Americans knew that we were uniquely blessed among peoples of the world; that there was a reason for this blessing, and attendant responsibility. Our norms and nobility now hang by a thread, yet as never in the past fifteen decades, millions of Americans sense the loss and want to do something about it.

Federal government has pushed Americans into Europe's trenches literally and figuratively since WWI. Each generation suffers additional regulations, permits, fees, fines, taxes, penalties, hidden cameras and tracking devices from birth until death; Big Brother tyranny as depicted in Orwell's *Nineteen Eighty-Four.*

In real life the predators are more subtle; coordinated political wolf-packs of corporations and also of teachers, social workers, librarians, mayors, city managers, school boards, county and State employees, lawyers, and consultants who attend Hawaii or Las Vegas workshops paid for by taxpayers, to learn how to control what you think and how to extract more tax dollars from you.

Predators have transformed a once-free republic into a dismal copy of Europe where citizens look to government for every aspect of existence from cradle to grave as they work to provide the bureaucrats with pensions and another round at the slot machines.

Farther down the rabbit hole

I will discuss the corporations presently; but first consider the extensive *hidden* predator, America's best kept business secret, the 501c3. The religious, political, legal, and economic think tanks and 'ministries' whose sincerity rivals that of the old crones who are hired to cry at Ukrainian funerals.

The Conservative movement that began with Barry Goldwater is now the Neoconservative camp, whose strange bedfellows include End Times prophets, the Israel-first lobby, the military-first subculture, the country-club progeny of Henry Clay, and befuddled Christians who can't find a better seat in electoral politics.

One would think that supporters of non-profits would wonder why their 501c3 seems to work on a 'crisis' for decades but never comes any closer to solving it. They don't grasp that one does not kill a goose that lays golden eggs. If you can whip up a donor's tears or anger, another tax-exempt $25, $50, $100 or sustaining $500 donation will follow. Donors' anxiety level must be kept high because for political and prophecy groups, crisis is a cash-cow. Circus mogul P.T. Barnum once said there's a sucker born every minute but presently in America, it's seven per minute.

All political flavors engage in this charade; it's the common ground for Al Gore, NRA, Pat Robertson, Greenpeace, CATO Institute, ACORN, Campaign for Liberty, Planned Parenthood, Heritage Foundation, Gays-R-Us, Pastor Israel's Prophecy Hotline, and hundreds more.

I am not referring to ministries that can be known by their fruits; feeding the hungry, clothing the naked, and giving a drink to the thirsty are missions worthy of support. There are other productive non-profits, as well. But the vast majority of them do nothing except subsist on your tax write-offs, knowing that you would rather funnel money to them than give it to the IRS. Their 'mission' accomplishes no measurable goals.

Don't misunderstand; I don't want you to think I have anything personal against your favorite non-profits; you're welcome to spend your money as you like. My purpose here is to have you understand *why things never improve* even though the 501c3s are constantly refilling your in-box and mailbox. If they perennially beg but never accomplish anything, you know that they're just another tug on your wallet for cotton candy.

As offensive as this assertion may appear to you, the stakes are high at present. If this parasite sector can keep you burdened with false crises, you will never make the time to think, to study, or to consider the causes and cures of America's *real* crises.

Lions, lions everywhere

A critical part of the predators' game is for the corporations and Congress to alternately pin blame on one another, and with both predators almost always blaming the IRS for life's hardships. Two generations of taxpayers bought this theater act, but Tax Honesty began making serious inroads beginning in the 1970s. Now, for tens of millions of us, the jig is up; the tactics by Congress and the corporations have been exposed. I will offer a vignette, and recommend David Korten's books for much more.

The mercantilists' clever commercial and military endeavor by which it has used Congress to enslave the American people – as both mercenary troops and as worker drones – harks back over a century. The cruel and inhuman emotional trauma of two world wars firmly established this working arrangement.

It is a simple fact of life that many well-respected people have been doing very immoral things for a very long time. Careers and industries hinge on maintaining the system as long as possible. Thus, for instance, when a citizen seeks to become a law-abiding Nontaxpayer, his or her HR manager will frame the request in terms of trouble and illegality; "I can't do that, it's illegal", or "We can't make special arrangements; the same paperwork for all".

In truth, it's nothing like that. American history through the past 50 years or so exhibits a clear demographic, industrial, and sociological shift into a new socialist-fascist balance. It is not only a corrupt Congress addicted to trillions; corporate America plays the game in the system because *it is half of the system.*

Public theater to the contrary, every fascist system follows the same arrangement; central government and the corporations move in symbiotic rhythm. As previously stated, Giovanni Gentile's classical definition of fascism in Mussolini's Italy has described America since at least Woodrow Wilson's administration.

The arrangement in fascist regimes is simple. It is Marx's plan in the Communist Manifesto, adjusted for private ownership of the means of production (as with the GM takeover, that is flexible, but usually the doctor owns his practice, but the government runs it; both work together to squeeze the prey).

The government trains citizens in K-12 schools, producing worker drones with no rational capacity, no historical framework, and no desire for independent inquiry. These workers always operate in groups at assigned tasks; they move smartly as a flock at the sound of the bell or horn. This nineteenth century Prussian sociology was promulgated by Horace Mann, John Dewey, and other inventors of modern government education.

The conditioning was perfected via two world wars, with the underlying social glue being the nationalism that always attends waving flags and flowing of our sons' blood. The allegiance to one's homeland (one's farm, community, or State) diminished as the pledge of allegiance to a fatherland took hold.

The specialization was not important – whether research, development, administration, line work, or military destruction of persons and property – government trained the troops for American corporations whose domestic and overseas assets require mercenaries and drone workers.

In return, the corporations skim the paychecks of all corporate workers, sending the trillions per year to Congress, the gatekeepers of the arrangement. As discussed last chapter, IRS is the black-hooded executioner, the middle man who takes the heat.

To the student of history, this fascism would be comical, were it not so horribly inhuman, and so butcherous to so many. But now the internet has presented a moral Rubicon to the world. While most of the world has crossed it, governments and large corporations will be the last to react. They will whistle in the dark and feed off the stragglers for as long as they can.

Various socialist/fascist arrangements are extant in most of the world. Citizens, especially the young and tech-savvy, will take note if AmericaAgain! succeeds. Governments and corporations have much to lose as this ancient mechanism is exposed, but as was the case for the Medieval guilds and monarchies as the *incunabulum* shifted everything: this is history, and it is inexorable.

Turn out the lights, the party's over

Despite all of the non-profits draining your emotions and occupying your brainspace every day, electoral politics is still the largest impediment to clear-headed self-government.

Citizens have attempted to arrest out-of-control government via politics for 175 years, and we've failed at the errand every time. Secession only divided us and made our enemies stronger. State nullification was a mark of desperation, not of sovereignty.

For years, a group called *We The People* led thousands of hens to march to the fox seeking redress of grievances, asking the fox to give hens a place at the table of politics. But he already *has* given hens a place – on his plate.

Now comes the Tea Party movement, acknowledging that the GOP is part of the problem, not a solution; but the GOP is attempting to co-opt this demonstration movement. If the GOP is successful, these Tea Parties will produce nothing beyond T-shirts, yard signs, and additional 'money bombs' for or against political candidates. Cotton candy, bunting, and party hats.

Life is not a party. A people who once knew to look to GOD to solve life's problems now looks to GOP for solutions in life. As explained in Chapter 9, political parties have been used to divide and conquer us for 150 years. Jerry Falwell, Pat Robertson, James Dobson et al support(ed) a party that has ravaged American liberty and our economy as much as the opposing party has done.

Praying to Almighty GOP

Before the god of politics consumed us, American life was risk, work, procreation, and raising one's children before the face of God. Life in America was about the pain, sweat, and much prayer of leadership; it was about raising children, crops, and animals with only an occasional glimpse of glory. It was making something out of cloth, steel, wood, glass, wire, or words that changed lives and made the effort worthwhile.

Life in America was making hard choices and letting your children see you do it; trusting God for another sunrise, another rain, and the strength to provide for your own – not trusting government or insurance companies to take life's risks away. We once knew what it was to be an American; it was good in our eyes and in the eyes of the world.

The political machine would have you dismiss all this; it would strip away the soul of civilization to gather us, witless and charmed, under festooned bunting for an unending string of political campaigns, and the Tea Party movement may be doing the same, every third weekend or so.

This Jacobin political activity cannot last. After years of emails, blast-faxes, mob rallies, pink slips and caravans, the political activist will feel that he lacks constitutional recourse; will abandon hope and be more deflated and inert than before, with a layer of cynicism added; the attitude of Europeans and Latin Americans.

The original Boston Tea Party lasted a few *hours,* after which the colonists moved on to war planning; not to money bombs to elect some of their number to British parliament.

The Tea Party movement has shown us the strength we have in numbers and the internet. Now it's time for duties beyond rallies; even beyond voting for statesmen. Our founders taught that citizen oversight alone will keep this republic. Elections are only a small fraction of our duty; elections have often brought change, but have never ushered in a *lasting,* positive change in American life.

A new view of your federal servant

As free citizens, our most important, most forgotten duty is to begin enforcing the Ninth and Tenth Amendments; bring criminals to justice *publicly and often, just as when we vote.* Being a law-abiding Nontaxpayer is only defense; our duty includes tactical offense.

If we adopt this sovereign citizen attitude, it will re-shape our way of life regarding our employees, which will improve their attitudes toward us. As Thomas Jefferson suggested, liberty exists wherever government fears its citizens.

Our Constitution enforced, at last

Citizens have never used courts of our sovereign States for a federal purpose, but a) collective defense vs. tyranny is the very meaning of the term *federal;* b) public corruption is the reason for grand juries; and c) as illustrated earlier, State trumps federal.

AmericaAgain! is an unprecedented Constitution-enforcement mechanism developed after four years of research and planning; a three-prong tactical plan meant to last as long as the Constitution. The proposed Texas HQ campus would be the People's own forward-deployed defense installation for the U.S. Constitution. Madison's Virginia Resolutions, tactically applied using the vertical check-and-balance described by Hamilton in Federalist #28.

The AmericaAgain! Indictment Engine™ will allow citizens to *enforce* the Ninth and Tenth Amendments in up to 535 State Courts across this republic for the first time. Whenever the public-private cartel engages in what appears to be suspicious activity, we enter that data in the politician's AmericaAgain! Indictment Engine™ file for targeting, passing it along to the local chapter to criminally indict their member of Congress in their own State Court.

Any twisting of the Interstate Commerce clause, General Welfare clause, or Necessary and Proper clause invites indictment on State charges such as criminal conspiracy, abuse of office, organized criminal activity, money laundering, legislative bribery, criminal solicitation, aggravated perjury, promoting a pyramid scheme, counterfeiting, and others. Threat of prison time and asset seizure will teach bent members of Congress the same lessons taught to Ken Lay and Bernie Madoff: crime no longer pays.

AmericaAgain! is the end of politics and the beginning of self-government mostly from home, on our terms.

The meaning of We The People

We have allowed public servants to treat the law as a joke; as with Mexican drug cartels, lawlessness is increasingly oppressive and frightening for producers. AmericaAgain! can present an equal-and-opposite frightening prospect to criminals.

Every power, program, office, department, agency, regulation, project, contract, and bureaucracy from birds to bulbs, from toilet flushes to tracing devices that is not *specifically* enumerated in Article I, Section 8 of the Constitution is illegal and must be defunded.

There is no doubt of the outcome if millions join the effort. The Supreme Law is on our side. Most of the enemy's funding is skimmed from our accounts; a third of citizens are already nonfilers and Tax Honesty is growing. We outnumber Congress *58,000-to-one* and numerical superiority means intellectual, logistical, and tactical superiority. We work from home, on our turf.

Moreover, God armeth the patriot: our armed county and State personnel can finally do their highest duty to preserve, protect, and defend the Constitution against domestic enemies. The bottom line must always be: *We The People remain in charge and responsible.*

As we put teeth in our long-abandoned supreme Law, we can begin to restore life free of predatory 'public servants'. We will shorten our creature's leash to allow it to reign only inside the ten-mile parcel on the Potomac that we granted it when we created it.

Financial Embargo: our most devastating weapon

The goal of the AmericaAgain! Tax Honesty Project™ is to inform citizens that for 97 years Congress has operated history's largest financial crime while pretending to complain about the Tax Code *that it wrote.* As millions more Taxpayers legally become Nontaxpayers, federal Leviathan must shrink, as must the billions of hours wasted annually on recordkeeping, avoidance, and compliance. Lower federal tax revenues will make public office less attractive to feckless parasites and more attractive to statesmen.

Dinosaurs in the tar pit

I cannot overstate the impact of AmericaAgain! if it succeeds; the first *vertical* check-and-balance mechanism by the People will fundamentally reorganize public life, overturn a long train of abuses, and restore the relationship stipulated in our Constitution.

Losers will be many, as we detailed above. As the internet increasingly empowers sovereign individuals, the two biggest losers are government bureaucracy and the federal law guild comprised of federal defenders and prosecutors, judges, U.S. supreme Court justices and staff, clerks, paralegals, functionaries, professors of constitutional law – and the extensive publishing, training, seminar, and accommodations industries supplying them.

Countless careers, estates, and reputations in a social order that began under the boots of Lincoln's federal troops, will be in peril. As in Medieval guilds, life has been good for its uniquely powerful players, and they will fight to save status quo; thus we must assure that our State Court players avoid intimidation or being bought off.

AmericaAgain! legal section will help local chapters bring cases initially in fleets; safety in numbers for State grand juries, prosecutors and judges. Our chapters will form groups of plaintiff citizens who, when their member of Congress is indicted, will stop marching outside the courthouse, and come inside to pack the courtroom, fill the halls, and pour out the front doors.

Regardless how *Tyrannosaurus Rex* may struggle in the tar, flailing his tiny forelegs and blinking his beady eyes in the harsh new sun, he cannot resist history. The federal law industry is no match for the inexorable power of the internet, liberating millions of citizens; a printing press on steroids, with wings.

Not an election cycle – a way of life

As self-governing Americans facing government corruption, we must see ourselves as the captain of a formerly mutinous crew. Yes, we face many foes as we take the helm again; but if we neglect our duty, worse things lie ahead. We've been accustomed to having politicians and media think for us and run our lives. Using the technology available to us all, AmericaAgain! will train citizens to oversee our politicians from home, as a new way of life.

The headquarters team

The AmericaAgain! HQ team through our legal section will design and maintain databases tracking and scoring every move made by your members of Congress. HQ legal section, using data collected by AmericaAgain! Liberty Labs™, will prepare bills of information and pre-indictment packages for local AmericaAgain! chapters and will work closely with volunteer legal teams in up to 535 American communities.

We plan to work with former sheriff Richard Mack and his Constitutional Sheriffs Association to assure that when a defendant member of Congress is in State custody, the defendant will remain in custody, not be sprung by cronies in federal government.

The James Madison Briefing Room™ will teach county and State judicial and law enforcement personnel their rights, powers, and duties under the U.S. Constitution; in Patrick Henry Hall™, AmericaAgain! members will learn this civics, also.

AmericaAgain! headquarters staff includes a video production team to clarify abstract subjects in constitutional law, civics, and history to inspire and equip self-governing sovereigns who lack the free time for heavy reading but can take in short, video-based lessons in civics and the Constitution.

With input from membership, our AmericaAgain! Legislative Action section will draft, refine, and push through passage of our targeted reform legislation, to roll back the unlawful federal actions of the past century. The AmericaAgain! Tax Honesty Project™ will teach citizens the history and law of Congress' largest financial fraud; offering education, not filing advice or services, with our national spokesman, former IRS-CID agent Joseph Banister.

In planning for four years, AmericaAgain! has only operated for a year as of this writing; our website launched on Thanksgiving 2009. Our team still has vacancies; when you visit our site, click on *Careers at AmericaAgain!* to determine whether you or someone you know may fit a need on our staff.

Man proposes, God disposes

Although some Americans believe that Mr. Obama is the end of the world, our slide into fascism began long ago. Since Lincoln's time, Americans have rejected God individually and as a culture. As the first chapter of Romans warns, God has given such people over to increasingly depraved sexual perversions, love for violence, and desire for profligate lifestyle. It is no small thing that 45 million Americans have been sacrificed by their parents on an altar to self.

America's founders achieved great exploits in settling these shores, forged a unique law and government and made a place in history by enduring hardship through faith.

Yes, our government has done us wrong, and for over 115 years it has done even worse to other peoples of the world. But government's sins are our fault as abdicating sovereigns; before making our servants repent their sins, we must humbly repent ours to our Great Sovereign.

Not since the Roosevelts have we seen arrogance in a president as in Barack Hussein Obama, but I see his push to a Marxist-fascist state as a blessing. Before his election, he promised his followers, *"five days from now we will fundamentally change America"*. He took his oath on a Bible used by Lincoln, and the irony is that fundamental change has been due since Lincoln's federal troops forged a new order in which *all* Americans have a master.

Now, the conservative part of America seethes with anger for the first time in generations about the activist federal courts, a ratcheting Big Brother police state, multi-billion-dollar payoffs to financial sector cronies, nationalized industries, an avowed Marxist winning the White House and working openly with a corrupt Congress to bring in further socialism. Our enemies believe they are on the verge of a new world order. I believe they have gone a bridge too far and lit new fire under a long-dormant population.

Is God sending this as the justice we deserve for generations of sin, or is He offering us a warning to repent so that He can show us mercy once more? In hopes of the latter, I invite you to join me in repentance, that the audacious Barack Hussein Obama may have his place in history – and we, ours.

Epilogue

The Bible stands, and it can rule our homes; the Constitution stands, and can again rule the public square. Our unique Supreme Law is *not* majority rule but rule of law; thus it need not be popular at first. The tactical beauty of AmericaAgain! is that a small minority can hold up the entire wall at this point, if we only will. Samuel Clemens, who used the pseudonym Mark Twain, said that,

> In the beginning of a change the patriot is a scarce man, and brave, and hated and scorned. When his cause succeeds, the timid join him, for then it costs nothing to be a patriot.

Clemens used *patriotism* in its classic sense; the love for one's hearth and home, for one's village, town, or perhaps State at most; never a huge, multifarious nation. Nationalism has ever only bred monsters waving flags and firing shots into the air. Like Jefferson and Madison, Clemens was stridently against blind nationalism, 'my country, right or wrong'. Thus he also said that "the only rational patriotism is loyalty to the nation all the time, but loyalty to the government only when it deserves it."

Our starting point must be to repent before the face of God. Repentance means to turn; to not repeat the sinful action that one has been committing.

AmericaAgain! membership will require little sacrifice from most of us; mostly a matter of checking on Congress as you check on the weather. If enough Americans join in, very few politicians will propose the sort of unconstitutional things they have proposed and perpetrated for the past 150 years. Some of us will go to our courthouse occasionally, to push through an indictment against a crime figure in Congress. Indictment Engine duty will pose less trouble than jury duty, yet will accomplish more for rule of law.

From over a decade of personal experience, I can tell you that an informed, law-abiding, self-governing citizen today is more free than our grandparents ever dreamed was possible.

Many books and websites today speak of conspiracies by the world's mega-predators. I have only briefly touched on the tactics used by individuals, families, and corporations who attempt to rule the world using governments as their stooges and national militaries as mercenaries to defend their worldwide assets. These evil ones will always exist in the world, and the subject is beyond the scope of this book. Yet I hope you realize that if a few million of us will repent, prepare, and work as AmericaAgain! members, we can cut the puppeteers' strings to Congress. That will be an historic and worthwhile attainment.

If life is all about money for them, it should not be so for us. No other place on earth is like America; appreciating this, living with our families in joy, and trusting God – these are our best defense against powerful, wicked men.

The U.S. Constitution is a singular law in history, with roots in *Magna Carta*, almost 800 years ago. If we would be patriots in the tradition of our forefathers, we must reclaim a Christian rule of law that dawned in the Runnymede valley on June 15, 1215 A.D. when Christian men thought like *Christians* and acted like *men*.

If you are serious about taking America back, then let's take it back; our Constitution stands ready for enforcement. Tea Party members have wanted to do *something* and I've demonstrated here that AmericaAgain! *is* that something.

This is not the republic and way of life that America's founders entrusted to us. If we quail at defending truth now, the beauty that men have made in imitating Christ will be as rare and fleeting as eclipses. When truth has gone out of the world, nothing can keep goodness from following truth, into the Old Dark. Then they will be seen only in nature; in small acts done in secret, and Scriptures left unread.

Let our children and their children see us begin here, now, to reclaim the faith of our ancestors, performing those duties with joy, for the time we have together under the sun.

Endnotes

Introduction

1. I capitalize *People* referring to citizens collectively and *State* because this is proper reference to sovereigns. I do not begin sentences with *federal* because I would have to capitalize it as federal players do. After 150 years of programming by our creature, we must return it to its place *in service to us,* the sovereign People and States.

2. Joseph T. Salerno, introduction to Murray N. Rothbard, *A History of Money and Banking in the United States* (von Mises Institute, 2002), 26-27.

3. Bill Bonner & Addison Wiggin, *Empire of Debt: The Rise of an Epic Financial Crisis* (John Wiley & Sons, 2006 Edition), 266.

4. I discuss The War to Enslave the States further in Chapter 9.

5. Regarding this other American reform movement, if you are weary of trained performers on Sunday instead of the one-another ministry seen in the New Testament, Google 'Frank Viola' or *Pagan Christianity.*

6. Ronald Reagan, 10/27/64 speech for the Barry Goldwater campaign.

Lie #1: The Constitution grants citizen rights

1. The book by former Idaho representative Phil Hart entitled *Constitutional Income: Do You Have Any?* is described in *Suggested Reading.* Also see Appendix D, *A Tax Honesty Primer,* to understand how Congress has defrauded you since your first paycheck.

2. For 17 additional government lies, see Andrew P. Napolitano, *Lies the Government Told You: Myth, Power, and Deception in American History* (Thomas Nelson 2010).

Lie #2: Supremacy Clause means federal trumps state

1. This language is from Madison's *Virginia Resolutions* and similar language in Jefferson's *Kentucky Resolutions*. Collectively, these works are known as the *Principles of '98.*

Lie #4: Sovereign immunity means Congress is untouchable

1. John Remington Graham, *Free, Sovereign and Independent States: The Intended Meaning of the American Constitution* (Pelican 2009), 307-308.

Lie #5: Everything is interstate commerce

1. Larry D. Kramer, *The People Themselves: Popular Constitutionalism and Judicial Review* (Oxford Univ. Press 2004) 247-248.

Lie #6: General welfare means the founders were socialists

1. Alexis deTocqueville, *Democracy in America,* Vol II, Part 4, Chap 6, *What Kind of Despotism Democratic Nations Have to Fear.*
2. February 7, 1792 missive written by Madison regarding Congressional regulation and subsidizing of the cod fishing industry.
3. Madison in his *Report on the Virginia Resolutions* (from the Virginia Delegation, related to the Alien and Sedition Acts) January, 1800.
4. Thomas Jefferson letter to Albert Gallatin dated June 16, 1817.

Lie #7: Voting is citizens' only remedy for corruption

1. The provenance of this old Texas cowboy song is unknown. When I was growing up on the Big O Ranch in the south Texas brush country, Dad had an album of Cowboy songs; this was one of my favorites.

Lie #8: The GOP is conservative

1. Andrew P. Napolitano, *The Constitution in Exile* (Thomas Nelson 2006) 75-76.

2. See Greg Loren Durand, *America's Caesar: The Decline and Fall of Republican Government in the United States of America* (Crown Rights Publishing, 2001) and its exhaustive list of primary source documents and other references about this uniquely monstrous president.

Lie #10: Congress can run domestic terror operations

1. Some members of Congress control far more than this as chairmen of committees. I do not wish to imply that *all* members of Congress are corrupt; only that all except for a tiny handful, do nothing to fight or expose the crimes being committed daily by Congress.

2. Under Chapter 2 (Lie #1) above, see note 1.

Suggested Resources

These men have taught me critical things. I believe they are all great men in their respective areas of endeavor. I've not met Frank or Gary, and only met Richard recently, but I'm profoundly impacted by the work of each of these fellows; seen their impact for Christ and the Constitution, occasionally at great price to them and their families. I don't agree with the theology or ecclesiology of all of them, but I love and value these men. After generations of social decomposition, God is sending work that signals *rebirth*. I heartily recommend their work to you.

Joseph Banister

The most courageous American I know, a veteran IRS-CID agent, Joe was attacked by the agency for being a whistleblower. After appearing on over 150 radio and television shows regarding the rogue agency, he was vindicated in court only after IRS had all but destroyed his family and CPA practice.

With the quiet demeanor of a sheepdog, Joe's dedication to truth and duty come across in word and action. We are honored to have this hero as our AmericaAgain! Tax Honesty Project™ spokesman. At the website www.freedomabovefortune.com his biography is available by clicking on that section.

Dave Champion

The nation's premiere Internet radio show host on Tax Honesty, Dave's book *Income Tax: Shattering the Myths,* will be available May 2010. Also a STIRLING Education advisor, I learned much about Tax Honesty over a decade from this courageous Christian and former military and SWAT officer.

Dave teaches tactical firearms at Front Sight Firearms Training Institute in Pahrump, NV. I consider his radio show – archives of which are available at www.davechampionshow.com – to have been the most important source of accurate information I found on Tax Honesty over the years. Dave's teaching covers Tax Honesty as well as the diverse areas of tactical firearms training, constitutional usurpation, and his take on news of the day.

Gary DeMar

I discovered Gary through his classic homeschooling history and worldview trilogy, *God & Government.* American Vision has a mission to *"make disciples (not just converts) of all nations and teach them to obey and apply the Bible to all of life"* (Matt. 28:18-20).

American Vision distributes resources designed to build and reinforce a Biblical worldview, helping Christians to engage and reclaim culture for Christ. Their website, www.americanvision.com offers reprints of forgotten, historically vital books as well as current books on strategically relevant subjects.

The Gary DeMar Show addresses religion, pop-culture, current events, and politics in a 15 minute daily online format. His American Vision website should be a saved link on your computer.

George Grant

A pastor in Franklin, Tennessee, Dr. Grant founded Franklin Classical School, directs King's Meadow Study Center, and is developing a 4-year Humanities curriculum that may one day rival the offering at St. John's College. George has written political books, *The Importance of the Electoral College, The Patriot's Handbook,* and *The Pocket Patriot,* history books such as *The Last Crusader: The*

Untold Story of Christopher Columbus, and also *The Blood of the Moon: Understanding the Historic Struggle Between Islam and Western Civilization,* and a Scottish history trilogy based on Sir Walter Scott's.

But as a D.Litt., George brings more to the table than interesting history and accurate civics; he paints the lessons in beautiful hues so they go down oh so easily. Any Shakespeare fan can attest to Robert Graves and Alan Hodge's assertion that "the writing of good English is...a moral matter", and so Dr. Grant's writing is above all, a moral enterprise in an age of rampant immorality. His book *Shelf Life: How Books Have Changed the Destinies and Desires of Nations* inspired me to write my book. His classic *The Micah Mandate* inspired me to follow Christ by a simple rule. Having written dozens of other books, several of them in collaboration with wife Karen, I think George may one day be seen as America's own C.S. Lewis, especially if the humanities degree program at King's Meadow Study Center succeeds. He has already achieved Lewis' rare gift; he draws men to Christ with beautiful use of the English language.

Richard Mack

The former sheriff of Graham County, Arizona, Richard works to restore the Constitution as the supreme law of the land by training sheriffs, constables, and other county and State peace officers to defend it in the face of federal tyranny.

In 1994, he and Montana sheriff Jay Printz filed a lawsuit challenging the Brady bill and won a U.S. Supreme Court ruling for States' rights. He's been interviewed on CNBC, Good Morning America, Donahue, Nightline, Crossfire, FOX News, and over 500 radio shows about his book *The County Sheriff: America's Last Hope.*

Richard is a consultant to lawyers and defendants in unlawful arrest and police misconduct cases. His www.sheriffmack.com site and books educate sheriffs, constables, and other peace officers to stand firm as the Constitution's last line of defense against tyranny.

Richard often appears with Yale Law graduate and former paratrooper Stewart Rhodes of www.oathkeepers.org, who teaches active-duty military, reserves, national guard, veterans, peace officers, and firefighters to fulfill their sworn oath to support and defend the Constitution against all enemies foreign and domestic.

R.C. Sproul, Jr.

The year I was born, Dr. Francis Schaeffer founded L'Abri Fellowship in Switzerland, which has transformed millions around the world, challenging Christians to think God's thoughts after Him; to live for Christ with one's whole being.

In 1971, R.C. Sproul founded Ligonier Valley Study Center to do much the same thing, with similar results here in America through the 'Reformed' community.

In 1996, R.C. Sproul Jr. founded Highlands Study Center in Mendota, Virginia and also planted St. Peter Presbyterian Church. R.C., Jr. has taught me a great deal about how to live simply, separately, and deliberately in Christ and with His saints, against all that the world teaches today. Their series of *Basement Tapes* and his other resources are found at www.highlandsministriesonline.org.

Frank Viola

First some background to set up my review of Frank Viola's world-changing work. Although many of the finest teachers today are of the Reformed stripe, I believe that the 'Reformation' was a political movement that fought alongside the Vatican to push simple Christ-followers into their system. In other words, I believe that the much-heralded 'Reformation' simply *wasn't*. As the Jerry Falwells and Pat Robertsons of their time, Luther and Calvin used politics to powerfully advance their popular causes.

Calvinists colonized America, so our church histories were written by the winners, a similar situation to all the propaganda you were taught about the War To Enslave The States. One must dig deep to find the truth about any period in history as compared to the popular version usually on the record thanks to the victors.

In 1974, while at university, Jesus Christ came into my life and overturned my Roman Catholic beliefs and traditions; Christ was the most wonderful thing in my life. But finding an honest fellowship of believers who follow Him in truth, against the culture – that was another matter entirely! By 1992, I had dragged my family through five denominations, seeking Christ in church meetings and Christian fellowship.

R.C. Sproul opened my eyes in many areas; my Southern Baptist churchianity was scripted, shallow, and unsatisfying. As explained above, his son R.C. Sproul Jr. went to simple, separate, deliberate life, closer to the New Testament model. So. Finally I could rest, I thought. I was all reformed and could go no 'higher' among the denominational flavors. You reach the top, there's Calvin in his slippers, awaiting you. Or so I was taught.

There were unsettling things about this 'reformed' faith. They sprinkled babies and call it Christian baptism; some of them wear a frock at a pulpit; they revere 'church fathers'; they keep religious traditions that relegate most of the adults to spectator status for life; they make teaching and preaching the Word into a learned, paid profession. What reformation? I was still back in Rome!

In the summer of 2003, I bought an old copy of Thielemann Van Braght's ancient classic *Martyrs Mirror*. As when I left the Vatican system, here I went again, learning truth about centuries-old traditions; the 'Reformation' as I learned, was a second front alongside the Vatican, coercing Christ-followers to join their political camp or die. Van Braght's *Martyrs Mirror* was another life-changing book for me – but not the last.

In 2005, I found an author who put it all together for me after my 30 year search; Frank Viola, a former public school teacher and 'house church' leader. Frank wrote *Pagan Christianity?: Exploring the Roots of our Church Practices* in 2003; for the second edition in 2008, he teamed up with George Barna and went with Tyndale House. Climbing high on Amazon's list, *Pagan Christianity?* shakes religious careerists to their foundations with such chapter titles as these:

- *Have We Really Been Doing It By The Book?*
- *The Church Building: Inheriting the Edifice Complex.*
- *The Order of Worship: Sunday Mornings Set In Concrete*

- *The Sermon: Protestantism's Most Sacred Cow*
- *The Pastor: Obstacle To Every-Member Functioning*
- *Sunday Morning Costumes: Covering Up The Problem*
- *Ministers of Music: Second-String Clergy*
- *Tithing and Clergy Salaries: Sore Spots On The Wallet*
- *Baptism and the Lord's Supper: Diluting The Sacraments*
- *Christian Education: Swelling The Cranium*
- *Reapproaching the New Testament: The Bible is not a Jigsaw Puzzle*
- *A Second Glance at the Savior: Jesus The Revolutionary*
- *The Next Step*
- *Final Thoughts: Q&A with Viola and Barna*

Frank's work goes farther; his other two vital books are listed in next section: *The Untold Story of the New Testament Church* and the sequel to Pagan Christianity, entitled *Finding Organic Church*.

I disagree with theological ideas in some of his other work, but these three books by Viola are among the most vital books in a millennium on the subjects of Scripture and how we should live as Christians. I warn you: Frank Viola's books will change your view of the Bible and of your church. If you're hungry for Christ and less churchianity, you'll love Frank Viola's work but your church's staff will not. Either learn and leave, or don't read Frank's books, but don't try to reform a denomination; they are an industry. And don't try to get a religious careerist to give up his paying gig; this leads to nothing but acrimony. You have been warned.

Douglas Wilson

One witnesses a Doug Wilson debate amazed at the fellow's Christ-likeness; tough and unyielding on principles, yet gracious and kind to debate opponents.

As the author of over 30 books, Doug was my earliest teacher in the theory and practice of applying classical Christian education within the institutional setting. In 1981, he and two friends founded Logos School in Moscow Idaho – a classical Christian school the curriculum for which modeled Dorothy Sayers' 1940s essay, *The Lost Tools of Learning*, describing the Medieval trivium.

Six years later, the group bought a roller rink and converted it to Logos School's permanent campus. Four years later, Doug wrote *Recovering the Lost Tools of Learning*, the book that changed my career direction and helped me to design Heritage Schools.

Doug has a rare combination: intellect, tenacity, and winsome personality. I never met a more sweet-spirited follower of Christ; yet he is a tenacious fighter for the faith. His is a life of accomplishment, besides Logos School, founding Christ Church, the assembly of which he is pastor; also the Association of Classical Christian Schools; Canon Press www.canonpress.org; New St. Andrews College, a Reformed version of the humanities program at St. John's College; and CREDENDA Agenda magazine, a trinitarian journal at www.credenda.org.

There is an amazing amount of hogswallop and snake oil being sold in America under two labels just now: *Christian* and *Patriot*. Of course, humanist hogswallop will always be a challenge, but we must reclaim these two words and what they once meant.

As I mentioned at the outset, I don't endorse any modern denomination's ecclesiology, or some of these brothers' theology on some points. If you're ready to grow up; to take up the difficult duties of an American and take on the difficult issues of a Christian, you can learn a great deal from the work of these men.

Suggested Reading

When someone asks me how I learned this stuff, I give them a reading list. Here, I list only title and author, not publisher or date because in most cases newer editions than mine are available. I could list thrice as many, but besides God's Word these are the books that I believe can give an American a grasp of why the world is as it is. These books won't make you an intellectual; read them with an open heart and they'll impart real wisdom. They are all great books, but I'll list my top 13 eye-opener books first.

A Baker's Dozen Eye-Opener Books

The Great Christian Revolution by Otto Scott demonstrates that no matter how they may balk, even the most heathen anti-Christian in the West is benefitting from centuries of Christian groundwork in every area of human endeavor.

Dismissing God by D. Bruce Lockerbie exposes the lives and work of the most influential writers of Abraham Lincoln's and at least four subsequent generations. Lockerbie explains how and why these angry humanists kicked out our moral underpinnings: Emily Dickinson, Walt Whitman, Ralph Waldo Emerson, Nathaniel Hawthorne, Herman Melville, Mark Twain, William Blake, Percy Bysshe Shelley, John Keats, John Ruskin, William Morris, William Butler Yeats, James Joyce, D.H Lawrence, Oscar Wilde, F. Scott Fitzgerald, and others including Ernest Hemingway. Here's the lineup of perpetrators used by America's schools to all but destroy our civilization, and Lockerbie's writing is beautiful, besides.

The Sovereign Individual by James Davidson & Lord William Rees-Mogg explains the shake-up of nations introduced by the Internet, as the printing press' impact on Medieval times. The world has not yet come to grips with the Internet, but a surprising amount of the turmoil in business and government is just that; the attempt by institutions to deal with this new way of life for humans. As the authors make clear, the individual and small business will come out the winners and big governments and institutions, the losers.

Constitutional Income: Do You have Any? by former Idaho Rep. Phil Hart, a professional engineer, is the meticulously-documented story of how Congress, from 1909-1913, conspired to produce the largest, longest-running financial crime in human history.

Lincoln Unmasked by Thomas J. DiLorenzo is a total debunking of the legends offered as reasons for Lincoln's war. The author exposes why Lincoln suspended *habeas corpus,* why he imprisoned *thousands* of Northern war dissenters and shut down *hundreds* of opposition newspapers. The author also exposes Lincoln's real economic agenda and if you wonder why you weren't taught this in school, see his chapters about Lincoln gatekeepers in academia and the appendix called *What They Don't Want You to Read.*

Overthrow: America's Century of Regime Change from Hawaii to Iraq by lifelong news correspondent Stephen Kinzer is the best single-volume historical survey of our government's attempts at empire. A quick read for those who don't like history, it puts the wars, islands, and faraway American real estate assets in perspective.

Red Republicans and Lincoln's Marxists: Marxism in the Civil War by Walter D. Kennedy and Al Benson, Jr. is a shocking account of the

Union army generals that were Marxist, and of the Marxist ideas that filled and characterized the Lincoln administration.

Reassessing the Presidency: The Rise of the Executive State and the Decline of Freedom is a 791-page lesson about how American history has been steered by our presidents; edited by John V. Denson. Each chapter can be read on its own, to better grasp a particular presidency or period of history. Taken together, it paints a clear picture of the recurring theme of Madison and Jefferson: presidents are not to be trusted; the People themselves must remain in control and vigilant.

The Costs of War: America's Pyrrhic Victories is another compendium edited by John Denson. A treasure-trove for those who want to learn why things are as they are in the world today. The book is worth buying for Ralph Raico's *Rethinking Churchill* chapter alone. Raico finally puts the Butcherous Bulldog of Britain in the hall of infamy alongside Lincoln, Teddy Roosevelt, and FDR.

Crossing the Rubicon: The Decline of the American Empire at the End of the Age of Oil by Michael C. Ruppert is the most professional and credible of 22 books and three videos I reviewed over eight years relating to the 9/11 debacle. I don't spend much time on the 911 debacle, and I only include this one book on that subject because that hoax catalyzed American domestic and foreign policy for the foreseeable future. Also Glenn Beck's churlish, insipid attacks on those who voice any disbelief in the government's story moved me to offer this detailed review as an open challenge to Mr. Beck.

As Erasmus of Rotterdam said, in the land of the blind, the one-eyed man is king. We needn't know everything about the 911 debacle; even a 4th grade child in possession of the facts will grasp that powerful men and institutions influence governments and have done, throughout history. The 150-year pattern in America since Fort Sumter is: a) we experience a catalyst attack either of unexplained origin, or out of proportion to the war that follows in response, then

b) federal government and its industry allies always ratchet their power during the process.

The term 'ratchet' used with respect to government arrogation is author Robert Higgs' way to describe the historical phenomenon of government gaining new ground against its own population or others, then holding that new ground to gain subsequent power. The one-way advance of tyranny.

My vision for AmericaAgain! is to beat the predator-parasite horde at their own game; self-governing citizens and resurgent sovereign States enforce the Constitution. Once we know how to end the pattern – when We The People have a firm legal choke-collar on every member of Congress – it makes no sense to argue about the last atrocity among many.

Whoever our domestic enemies may be, we know that they must use Congress for financing and for legislative enablement. After every war, they've kept us arguing amongst ourselves for decades about who or what caused the fire, rather than allowing us time to think and build safeguards against theft by those that caused the fires only for distraction.

Whatever the hoax or the modus, these players' goal is always to become seriously, insanely wealthy; Congress is their conduit, and the blood and destruction of war is just added color. Butcherous hoaxes leading us into wars will continue to succeed until a critical mass of the People get a clue and develop a lasting counterforce like the AmericaAgain! mechanism.

This book is on my top dozen eye-openers list because the government's preposterous story and its media hacks should be hooted off the stage. Despite his other meritorious ideas, Glenn Beck has been a gullible 'useful idiot' on this issue.

As for the particulars: I'm one of several hundred engineers, scientists, and architects signed on to a list at *Architects and Engineers for 911 Truth* not because I care to argue specifics of this latest in the long pattern of war-sparking hoaxes. I joined that list because the official story is just so preposterous with respect to structural forensics, physics, materials science and the history of structural failures as to make us appear a nation of idiots, in falling for it.

As a professional engineer having performed structural design for two decades, I became interested in this hoax from the first few seconds of video I watched of WTC tower collapses that morning. To assert with a straight face that the first three instances in history of fire-induced structural collapse of steel multistory buildings occurred in one city, in one day – one of them having no aircraft collision around which to concoct a story – is simply ludicrous.

There have been dozens of raging fires in steel structures around the world. Some lasted much longer than the WTC fires, yet none led to plastic collapse, much less to the pulverizing, free-fall-velocity collapse mode seen thrice on 911 and never witnessed before or since – except in *every* controlled demolition.

Occam's Razor holds that the simplest explanation is the most likely; if the evidence contradicts an explanation that demands addition of unlikely assumptions, that explanation is likely untrue.

Moreover, on the morning of July 28, 1945, a fully-fueled B-25 Mitchell bomber lost in fog over Manhattan slammed into the 79th floor of the Empire State Building. The structure sustained no lasting damage, much less did it collapse. Much less did it exhibit the free-fall-velocity, symmetrical axial implosion failure mode seen in steel structures *only* in controlled demolition.

This mass stupidity on parade with Glenn Beck as its latest poster-boy just cries for rational public response and, among all the 911 books I found, Ruppert's is the best because unlike most of the others, it goes to the root. The geopolitical forces in play in all world mega-events are there because such things require phenomenal amounts of money, logistics, and coordination that only major financial players can bring to bear. The idea that the bungling Bush administration could have done it alone or with help from a handful of Muslim fundamentalists, is preposterous.

It's one thing to believe sepia-tone legends about 'Honest Abe' because you learned them all through school; it's another thing to believe this preposterous story that defies all logic and evidence, just because the insipid masses may jeer.

To be perfectly blunt, the long 911 debacle, as was also true of the 20-year-long 'Who really killed Kennedy?' argument, prove that most Americans are easily duped by distractions, and seriously in need of remedial history, civics, and logic.

Pagan Christianity?: Exploring the Roots of our Church Practices, by Frank Viola and George Barna is a tough one for this list. This is a very dangerous book, as I said in the *Suggested Resources* section about Frank. If you have felt empty or useless in your walk with Christ, this book will cause a crisis of conscience and of action. If you're prepared to search for a New Testament body of believers and quietly leave the place where you now 'attend', then read this book. But *do not* read it if you'd be tempted to take it up with paid church staff; that can only end bitterly. Christianity, Inc. is definitely not open to reforming its way out of business.

The Untold Story of the New Testament Church also by Frank Viola explains how trying to read the Bible in the order we have it today is like re-arranging all the chapters of a novel, binding it back together, then trying to make sense of the story. One of the most fascinating books I've ever read.

Finding Organic Church: A Comprehensive Guide to Starting and Sustaining Authentic Christian Communities my third favorite by Frank Viola explains how to gather with other believers in an organic fellowship, without repeating the 501c3 lunacy of Christianity, Inc. or the opposite lunacy of most short-lived 'house church' startups. Viola brings many years of hard experiences – his and those of many others who have given him input as Frank Viola has become a major figure in modern reformation. Before you try it, understand that this is very hard work, and not for everyone.

The Balance of My Suggested Reading List

President Who?: Forgotten Founders by Stanley L. Klos was one of those eye-opener books in my life. George Washington called Peyton Randolph *"Father of our country"* because Randolph was the first President of the United States in Congress Assembled – and nine other presidents filled that post prior to George Washington. See? I wasn't kidding; you were cheated in your education.

Free, Sovereign, and Independent States: The Intended Meaning of the American Constitution by John Remington Graham explains the U.S. Constitution one sentence at a time, tracing the legislative history from the king's courts and parliament of Great Britain up to the constitutional convention. This is a ready reference on every clause in the Constitution; if you seek more in-depth treatment and if you have the shelf space, the 5-volume set *The Founders' Constitution* by editors Kurland and Lerner, includes extracts from leading works of political theory, history, law, and constitutional argument that the Framers and their contemporaries used and produced. I believe a CD version is forthcoming; that will be much handier.

Empire of Debt by Bill Bonner and Addison Wiggin trace America's past 120 years of world conquest, measuring blood and money with a delightful mix of humor and morose fact that keeps you turning the pages to find out how stupid we can get before we wise up. This is a modern classic that leaves no doubt about how America has become what we are today.

The Republic of Letters: The Correspondence Between Jefferson and Madison 1776-1826 a 3-volume compendium of 50 years' correspondence between the two giants among America's founding fathers. Series editor James Smith segues the correspondence with commentary that helps the reader notice these men's development over their lifetimes. I learned more about James Madison from these letters than from seven Madison biographies. To really grasp a man's thinking over time, read his letters.

The People Themselves: Popular Constitutionalism and Judicial Review by Larry D. Kramer, dean of the Stanford Law School, is no dry tome of constitutional law; it's a refreshing look into why we should do exactly what I'm proposing with the AmericaAgain! mechanism.

Ideas Have Consequences by Richard M. Weaver is an amazing little classic the thesis of which is that language, virtue, maleness, femaleness, and ancient mores have almost gone out of the world. Weaver ends on a somber note that I disagree with; but this book made me think about truth, goodness, and beauty outside my old religious categories, as they are in the universe that God has made.

Democracy in America by Alexis deTocqueville is a classic work of economics, sociology, and political science. Although he does not come to grips with the republican form of government entailed in our Constitution, Tocqueville was prescient about *democracy* in America. In other words, the founders would have agreed; the representative, constitutional republic of sovereign States as they designed it was intended to avoid *democracy*, or rule of the majority. Founders often inveighed against democracy as among the worst.

Still, from the limited view of a Frenchman, Tocqueville saw that democracy would degenerate into 'soft despotism', precisely the case today. He predicted tyranny of the majority as James Madison had warned about 50 years before.

As quoted on page 35 above, Tocqueville was also correct that a majoritarian tyranny would spring from the confluence of two factors: dependence on government for material security, and the growing prejudices of an ignorant mass. The effect of 150 years of government education is that most citizens are not only unfit to rule themselves, but unfit to oversee their creature government, instead begging it for provision and security.

<u>*Economics in One Lesson*</u> by Henry Hazlitt is an acknowledged little classic; an economics primer for people like me who hated accounting and economics subjects in college, but who really needed to know how labor, money, government, and credit operate in society to cause wars, inflation, depressions, and such.

<u>*A History of Money and Banking in the United States*</u> by Murray N. Rothbard, a student of Ludwig von Mises who was a founder of Austrian School economics. Rothbard unabashedly shows where the bodies were buried as bankers and Washington D.C. debased and despoiled our currency from the colonial era to World War II.

<u>*The Case Against the Fed*</u> by Rothbard is a much smaller book with a much more practical goal: to show how Americans can shut down the longest-running counterfeiting scam in history. This work forms the basic guide for the design of the AmericaAgain! legislation to be called *The Lawful American Currency and Banking Act.*

<u>*Blood Money: The Civil War and the Federal Reserve*</u> by John Remington Graham explains that the Federal Reserve scam began two generations before the Jekyll Island gang and Congress teamed up in 1913 to begin blindfolding and gang-raping the People.

<u>*Barbara Villiers or, A History of Monetary Crimes*</u> by Alexander del Mar is a tiny book with a misleading name. Villiers was a favored mistress of an English king, for whose personal benefit coinage laws were passed. If you think this bizarre, read Rothbard's history, cited above; American monetary legislation since Lincoln's time has been the same kind of deals but with *many* 'mistresses'.

<u>*America's Caesar: The Decline and Fall of Republican Government in the United States of America*</u> by Greg L. Durand probes more deeply than does DiLorenzo into the personal and religious aspects of Lincoln's character, using primary-source documentation to prove that Lincoln was the moral mixture of Bill Clinton and Saddam

Hussein: a slick, godless butcher with a pious public persona. Read these quotes from his friends, contemporaries, and Lincoln's own pen. Yes, you received a propagandist education.

Destroying the Republic: Jabez Curry and the Re-Education of the Old South by John Chodes is the story of Jabez Curry's transformation from an Alabama aristocrat and supporter of State sovereignty, into a federal bureaucrat and executive of the Peabody Education Fund, one of several national funds that emasculated Southern and agrarian culture in America, rendering the population more easily molded into corporate drones. Tracing Curry's moral descent in exchange for a place at the table with 'big boys', the book exposes the moral retrogression of the government schools.

Churchill's Folly: How Winston Churchill created modern Iraq is the back story by Christopher Catherwood, of Britain's dissection of the Persian empire to create a site for the petrodollar bloodbath we've seen ever since. Ralph Raico's wonderful chapter called *Rethinking Churchill* in the book *Reassessing the Presidency* reviewed above removed my blinders about the old 'bulldog' whose clever turns of phrase had always captured me. In this book, I learned just what a scheming, immoral politician he actually was.

It's the Crude, Dude: Greed, Gas, War, and the American Way by Linda McQuaig is a well-documented history of America's portion of that same game played by the British and French, in the sands of Araby.
  It's one of those books that first made me so furious about the 'military industrial complex' that I wanted to just give up – and then came AmericaAgain!, and hope of cutting the puppeteer's strings that have controlled our Congress for over 150 years. This book does evoke a great deal of sympathy for any of the Middle East peoples, as long as big petroleum owns Congress.

Wilson's War: How Woodrow Wilson's Great Blunder led to Hitler, Lenin, Stalin & World War II by Jim Powell is an excellent primer on

Tom 'Woodrow' Wilson, highlighting the milquetoast do-gooder's colossal blunders from Mexico to Venezuela to Europe's two world wars. Reading this account of presidential incompetence such as many other presidents have since mimicked, helped me to finally understand that it wasn't incompetence so much as useful, stupid complicity; and finally I saw why the federal government dragged the American People into Europe's world wars.

FDR's Folly: How Roosevelt and his New Deal prolonged the Great Depression is the second primer on America's world-war presidents by historian Jim Powell. As he does with Wilson, the author here illustrates how mendacious and bungling FDR was. The hero of my parents' generation was a friend of Stalin, who killed 20 million of his own people; but this book proves that beyond being evil, FDR was a blithering fool.

Roosevelt's Secret War: FDR & World War II Espionage is the story of FDR's creation of America's intelligence network. Author Joseph Persico says, "Few leaders were better adapted temperamentally to espionage than FDR; (he) compartmentalized information, misled associates, manipulated people, conducted intrigues, used private lines of communication, scattered responsibility, duplicated assignments, provoked rivalries, held the cards while showing few, and left few fingerprints." And this from an author that *likes* FDR, referring to him as a principled Machiavellian who hoped to achieve several clear ends (i.e., getting America into WWII) although most Americans wanted nothing to do with it before Pearl Harbor.

Day of Deceit: The Truth about FDR and Pearl Harbor is Robert B. Stinnett's copious proof showing that indeed, Pearl Harbor was not a surprise to FDR; it was just the "911" that the devious FDR needed to prime the billion-dollar war machine on both sides of the ocean, to supposedly create millions of new jobs. So what's a few tens of thousands dead, right? As is the case with Persico, Stinnett is still supportive of FDR, but in reporting what he has found, we see plenty of smoking guns placing FDR as the useful puppet of the military-industrial complex almost a generation before President Eisenhower coined the term.

Constitutional Chaos: What Happens When the Government Breaks its Own Laws by Fox News Senior Judicial Analyst and former New Jersey Superior Court Judge Andrew P. Napolitano is the first book I would read by this trenchant jurist if you'd like to unfold the story of our constitutional crisis in stages. Appalling.

The Constitution in Exile: How the federal government has seized power by rewriting the Supreme Law of the Land might be called an atrocity update, written in 2006, two years after the abovementioned book and covers much of the same ground. This one by Judge Napolitano is even more appalling than the other.

Lies the Government Told You: Myth, Power, and Deception in American History is perhaps Judge Napolitano's best work yet; a list of 17 lies by which the federal Leviathan keeps citizens on their leashes, versus the other way around, which was the Founders' intention. While none of Judge Napolitano's solutions come close to matching the efficacy of AmericaAgain!, he is the most honest jurist writing and speaking publicly today in America, about the moral bankruptcy of the federal government including its courts.

The Beast on the East River: The U.N. Threat to America's Sovereignty and Security by Nathan Tabor, founder of TheConservativeVoice. com, is the best analysis of the U.N. threat that I have read. We used this book to draft the sections of the AmericaAgain! Declaration that deal with the U.N. debacle.

The Harsh Truth About Public Schools by homeschooling Houston attorney Bruce N. Shortt, Texas coordinator for Exodus Mandate. He and his wife homeschool their own children, but Bruce was so shocked as he investigated the public schools that he felt compelled to write this shocking investigative report to warn parents whose children are enrolled in them. Bruce has reported over the years since publishing this book that things have only gotten worse. This book should have alerted you to the failure of government schools to teach honest history or any civics at all; but if your children are enrolled in them, it's your parental duty to know the emotional trauma they face there as well.

Income Tax: Shattering the Myths by David A. Champion has just gone to press; I haven't read it yet. However, Dave is the person I most trust in the Tax Honesty movement so I recommend this book without reservation, having known him for eight years.

Unaccountable: How the accounting profession forfeited a public trust by Mike Brewster takes you from ancient clay tablets in Sumeria up to the breakup of the Big Eight, in a fast-moving tale of deceit and unprofessionalism, making 'the dismal profession' a riveting read.

Martyrs Mirror by Thielemann van Braght is a massive, hardbound compendium of 16 centuries of martyrs for the faith, from the apostles of Christ, through the time of the supposed 'Reformation', when plain believers who refused to sprinkle their babies and call it baptism were financially ruined, run out of town, jailed indefinitely and left to starve, drowned, or burned to death by Roman Catholics, Lutherans, and Calvinists. The purpose of reviewing all these senseless murders is to see that: a) Christians have been as savage in the past as Mohammedans, in the name of religion; b) the 'Reformation' is history's most accepted, well-disguised political fraud; and c) those of the 'Reformed' faith run from confronting these facts just as Roman Catholics run from confronting the Spanish Inquisition, and just as those whose careers depend on Congress' IRS scam, run from the evidence for Tax Honesty.

I find it fascinating that a free people can bury history's mega-frauds even after they're introduced to them. But many people do it anyway, thinking that by putting the subject out of mind, it will just go away. Instead, these things have a way of coming back to kill you – or your children or grandchildren, when they are far less able to defend themselves than we are today.

Join AmericaAgain! and then I say, take up and read. Before any of the listed books, read Appendices C and D, in the following section. Each of them should only be read after you've had time to digest the body of this book; realize that most of this civics is unknown today to most State judges and prosecutors, and to most of your representatives in the State and federal legislatures. We are simply an ignorant people at this point; but ignorance is curable; that's why I always say, "Take up and read!"

Appendix C and D are each a standalone study of some hours, but if you will tackle them with a heart dedicated to forging a new future for our republic, just in your own household and neck of the woods, then the appendices will be worth the time you invest in grasping them. We have work to do, and thank God we yet have the freedom to do it.

Appendices

Appendix A:

The Declaration of Independence

In CONGRESS, July 4, 1776

The Unanimous Declaration of the thirteen united States of America

When, in the course of human events, it becomes necessary for one people to dissolve the political bonds which have connected them with another, and to assume among the powers of the earth, the separate and equal station to which the laws of nature and of nature's God entitle them, a decent respect to the opinions of mankind requires that they should declare the causes which impel them to the separation.

We hold these truths to be self-evident, that all men are created equal, that they are endowed by their Creator with certain unalienable rights, that among these are life, liberty and the pursuit of happiness.

That to secure these rights, governments are instituted among men, deriving their just powers from the consent of the governed.

That whenever any form of government becomes destructive to these ends, it is the right of the people to alter or to abolish it, and to institute new government, laying its foundation on such principles and organizing its powers in such form, as to them shall seem most likely to effect their safety and happiness.

Prudence, indeed, will dictate that governments long established should not be changed for light and transient causes; and accordingly all experience hath shown that mankind are more disposed to suffer, while evils are sufferable, than to right themselves by abolishing the forms to which they are accustomed.

But when a long train of abuses and usurpations, pursuing invariably the same object evinces a design to reduce them under absolute despotism, it is their right, it is their duty, to throw off such government, and to provide new guards for their future security.

Such has been the patient sufferance of these colonies; and such is now the necessity which constrains them to alter their former systems of government. The history of the present King of Great Britain is a history of repeated injuries and usurpations, all having in direct object the establishment of an absolute tyranny over these states. To prove this, let facts be submitted to a candid world.

He has refused his assent to laws, the most wholesome and necessary for the public good.

He has forbidden his governors to pass laws of immediate and pressing importance, unless suspended in their operation till his assent should be obtained; and when so suspended, he has utterly neglected to attend to them.

He has refused to pass other laws for the accommodation of large districts of people, unless those people would relinquish the right of representation in the legislature, a right inestimable to them and formidable to tyrants only.

He has called together legislative bodies at places unusual, uncomfortable, and distant from the depository of their public records, for the sole purpose of fatiguing them into compliance with his measures.

He has dissolved representative houses repeatedly, for opposing with manly firmness his invasions on the rights of the people.

He has refused for a long time, after such dissolutions, to cause others to be elected; whereby the legislative powers, incapable of annihilation, have returned to the people at large for their exercise;

the state remaining in the meantime exposed to all the dangers of invasion from without, and convulsions within.

He has endeavored to prevent the population of these states; for that purpose obstructing the laws for naturalization of foreigners; refusing to pass others to encourage their migration hither, and raising the conditions of new appropriations of lands.

He has obstructed the administration of justice, by refusing his assent to laws for establishing judiciary powers.

He has made judges dependent on his will alone, for the tenure of their offices, and the amount and payment of their salaries.

He has erected a multitude of new offices, and sent hither swarms of officers to harass our people, and eat out their substance.

He has kept among us, in times of peace, standing armies without the consent of our legislature.

He has affected to render the military independent of and superior to civil power.

He has combined with others to subject us to a jurisdiction foreign to our constitution, and unacknowledged by our laws; giving his assent to their acts of pretended legislation:

For quartering large bodies of armed troops among us:

For protecting them, by mock trial, from punishment for any murders which they should commit on the inhabitants of these states:

For cutting off our trade with all parts of the world:

For imposing taxes on us without our consent:

For depriving us in many cases, of the benefits of trial by jury:

For transporting us beyond seas to be tried for pretended offenses:

For abolishing the free system of English laws in a neighboring province, establishing therein an arbitrary government, and enlarging its boundaries so as to render it at once an example and fit instrument for introducing the same absolute rule in these colonies:

For taking away our charters, abolishing our most valuable laws, and altering fundamentally the forms of our governments:

For suspending our own legislatures, and declaring themselves invested with power to legislate for us in all cases whatsoever.

He has abdicated government here, by declaring us out of his protection and waging war against us.

He has plundered our seas, ravaged our coasts, burned our towns, and destroyed the lives of our people.

He is at this time transporting large armies of foreign mercenaries to complete the works of death, desolation and tyranny, already begun with circumstances of cruelty and perfidy scarcely paralleled in the most barbarous ages, and totally unworthy the head of a civilized nation.

He has constrained our fellow citizens taken captive on the high seas to bear arms against their country, to become the executioners of their friends and brethren, or to fall themselves by their hands.

He has excited domestic insurrections amongst us, and has endeavored to bring on the inhabitants of our frontiers, the merciless Indian savages, whose known rule of warfare, is undistinguished destruction of all ages, sexes and conditions.

In every stage of these oppressions we have petitioned for redress in the most humble terms: our repeated petitions have been answered only by repeated injury. A prince, whose character is thus marked by every act which may define a tyrant, is unfit to be the ruler of a free people.

Nor have we been wanting in attention to our British brethren. We have warned them from time to time of attempts by their legislature to extend an unwarrantable jurisdiction over us. We have reminded them of the circumstances of our emigration and settlement here. We have appealed to their native justice and magnanimity, and we have conjured them by the ties of our common kindred to disavow these usurpations, which, would inevitably interrupt our connections and correspondence. They too have been deaf to the voice of justice and of consanguinity. We must, therefore, acquiesce in the necessity, which denounces our separation, and hold them, as we hold the rest of mankind, enemies in war, in peace friends.

We, therefore, the representatives of the United States of America, in General Congress, assembled, appealing to the Supreme Judge of the world for the rectitude of our intentions, do, in the name, and by the authority of the good people of these colonies, solemnly publish and declare, that these united colonies are, and of right ought to be free and independent states; that they are absolved from all allegiance to the British Crown, and that all political connection between them and the state of Great Britain, is and ought to be totally dissolved; and that as free and independent states, they have full power to levy war, conclude peace, contract alliances, establish commerce, and to do all other acts and things which independent states may of right do. And for the support of this declaration, with a firm reliance on the protection of Divine Providence, we mutually pledge to each other our lives, our fortunes and our sacred honor.

Appendix B:

The U.S. Constitution

We the People of the United States, in Order to form a more perfect Union, establish Justice, insure domestic Tranquility, provide for the common defence, promote the general Welfare, and secure the Blessings of Liberty to ourselves and our Posterity, do ordain and establish this Constitution for the United States of America.

Article I.

Section 1. All legislative Powers herein granted shall be vested in a Congress of the United States, which shall consist of a Senate and House of Representatives.

Section 2. The House of Representatives shall be composed of Members chosen every second Year by the People of the several States, and the electors in each State shall have the qualifications requisite for electors of the most numerous branch of the State legislature.

No Person shall be a Representative who shall not have attained to the Age of twenty five Years, and been seven Years a citizen of the

United States, and who shall not, when elected, be an Inhabitant of that State in which he shall be chosen.

Representatives and direct Taxes shall be apportioned among the several States which may be included within this Union, according to their respective Numbers, which shall be determined by adding to the whole number of free Persons, including those bound to Service for a Term of Years, and excluding Indians not taxed, three fifths of all other Persons. The actual Enumeration shall be made within three Years after the first Meeting of the Congress of the United States, and within every subsequent Term of ten Years, in such Manner as they shall by law Direct. The number of Representatives shall not exceed one for every thirty Thousand, but each State shall have at least one Representative; and until such enumeration shall be made, the State of New Hampshire shall be entitled to chuse three, Massachusetts eight, Rhode Island and Providence Plantations one, Connecticut five, New York six, New Jersey four, Pennsylvania eight, Delaware one, Maryland six, Virginia ten, North Carolina five, South Carolina five, and Georgia three.

When vacancies happen in the Representation from any State, the Executive Authority thereof shall issue Writs of Election to fill such Vacancies.

The House of Representatives shall chuse their Speaker and other Officers; and shall have the sole Power of Impeachment.

Section 3. The Senate of the United States shall be composed of two Senators from each State, chosen by the legislature thereof, for six Years; and each Senator shall have one Vote.

Immediately after they shall be assembled in Consequence of the first Election, they shall be divided as equally as may be into three Classes. The Seats of the Senators of the first Class shall be vacated at the expiration of the second Year, of the second Class at the expiration of the fourth Year, and of the third Class at the expiration of the sixth Year, so that one third may be chosen every second Year; and if vacancies happen by Resignation, or otherwise, during the recess of the Legislature of any State, the Executive thereof may make temporary Appointments until the next meeting of the Legislature, which shall then fill such Vacancies.

No person shall be a Senator who shall not have attained to the Age of thirty Years, and been nine Years a Citizen of the United States, and who shall not, when elected, be an Inhabitant of that State for which he shall be chosen.

The Vice-President of the United States shall be President of the Senate, but shall have no Vote, unless they be equally divided.

The Senate shall choose their other Officers, and also a President pro tempore, in the Absence of the Vice-President, or when he shall exercise the Office of President of the United States.

The Senate shall have the sole Power to try all Impeachments. When sitting for that Purpose, they shall be on Oath or Affirmation. When the President of the United States is tried, the Chief Justice shall preside: And no Person shall be convicted without the Concurrence of two thirds of the Members present.

Judgment in cases of Impeachment shall not extend further than to removal from Office, and disqualification to hold and enjoy any Office of honor, Trust or Profit under the United States: but the Party convicted shall nevertheless be liable and subject to Indictment, Trial, Judgment and Punishment, according to Law.

Section 4. The Times, Places and Manner of holding Elections for Senators and Representatives, shall be prescribed in each State by the Legislature thereof; but the Congress may at any time by Law make or alter such Regulations, except as to the Places of chusing Senators.

The Congress shall assemble at least once in every Year, and such Meeting shall be on the first Monday in December, unless they shall by law appoint a different Day.

Section 5. Each House shall be the Judge of the Elections, Returns and Qualifications of its own Members, and a Majority of each shall constitute a Quorum to do Business; but a smaller Number may adjourn from day to day, and may be authorized to compel the Attendance of absent Members, in such Manner, and under such Penalties as each House may provide.

Each house may determine the Rules of its Proceedings, punish its Members for disorderly Behavior, and, with the Concurrence of two-thirds, expel a Member.

Each house shall keep a Journal of its Proceedings, and from time to time publish the same, excepting such Parts as may in their Judgment require Secrecy; and the Yeas and Nays of the Members of either House on any question shall, at the Desire of one fifth of those Present, be entered on the Journal.

Neither House, during the Session of Congress, shall, without the Consent of the other, adjourn for more than three days, nor to any other Place than that in which the two Houses shall be sitting.

Section 6. The Senators and Representatives shall receive a Compensation for their Services, to be ascertained by Law, and paid out of the Treasury of the United States. They shall in all Cases, except Treason, Felony and Breach of the Peace, be privileged from Arrest during their Attendance at the Session of their respective Houses, and in going to and returning from the same; and for any Speech or Debate in either House, they shall not be questioned in any other Place.

No Senator or Representative shall, during the Time for which he was elected, be appointed to any civil Office under the authority of the United States, which shall have been created, or the Emoluments whereof shall have been increased during such time; and no Person holding any Office under the United States, shall be a Member of either House during his Continuance in Office.

Section 7. All Bills for raising Revenue shall originate in the House of Representatives; but the Senate may propose or concur with Amendments as on other Bills.

Every Bill which shall have passed the House of Representatives and the Senate, shall, before it become a Law, be presented to the President of the United States; If he approve he shall sign it, but if not he shall return it, with his Objections to that House in which it shall have originated, who shall enter the Objections at large on their Journal, and proceed to reconsider it.

If after such Reconsideration two thirds of that house shall agree to pass the Bill, it shall be sent, together with the Objections, to the other House, by which it shall likewise be reconsidered, and if approved by two thirds of that House, it shall become a law. But in all such Cases the Votes of both Houses shall be determined by Yeas and Nays, and the Names of the Persons voting for and against the Bill shall be entered on the Journal of each House respectively.

If any Bill shall not be returned by the President within ten Days (Sundays excepted) after it shall have been presented to him, the Same shall be a Law, in like Manner as if he had signed it, unless the Congress by their Adjournment prevent its Return, in which case it shall not be a Law.

Every Order, Resolution, or Vote to which the Concurrence of the Senate and House of Representatives may be necessary (except on a question of Adjournment) shall be presented to the President of the United States; and before the Same shall take Effect, shall be approved by him, or being disapproved by him, shall be repassed by two thirds of the Senate and House of Representatives, according to the Rules and Limitations prescribed in the Case of a Bill.

Section 8. The Congress shall have Power to lay and collect Taxes, Duties, Imposts and Excises, to pay the Debts and provide for the common Defence and general Welfare of the United States; but all Duties, Imposts and Excises shall be uniform throughout the United States;

To borrow Money on the credit of the United States;

To regulate Commerce with foreign Nations, and among the several States, and with the Indian Tribes;

To establish an uniform Rule of Naturalization, and uniform Laws on the subject of Bankruptcies throughout the United States;

To coin Money, regulate the Value thereof, and of foreign Coin, and fix the Standard of Weights and Measures;

To provide for the Punishment of counterfeiting the Securities and current Coin of the United States;

To establish Post Offices and Post Roads;

To promote the Progress of Science and useful Arts, by securing for limited Times to Authors and Inventors the exclusive Right to their respective Writings and Discoveries;

To constitute Tribunals inferior to the supreme Court;

To define and punish Piracies and Felonies committed on the high Seas, and Offenses against the Law of Nations;

To declare War, grant Letters of Marque and Reprisal, and make Rules concerning Captures on Land and Water;

To raise and support Armies, but no Appropriation of Money to that Use shall be for a longer term than two Years;

To provide and maintain a Navy;

To make Rules for the Government and Regulation of the land and naval Forces;

To provide for calling forth the Militia to execute the Laws of the Union, suppress Insurrections and repel Invasions;

To provide for organizing, arming, and disciplining, the Militia, and for governing such Part of them as may be employed in the Service of the United States, reserving to the States respectively, the Appointment of the Officers, and the Authority of training the militia according to the discipline prescribed by Congress;

To exercise exclusive Legislation in all Cases whatsoever, over such District (not exceeding ten Miles square) as may, by Cession of particular States, and the Acceptance of Congress, become the Seat of the Government of the United States, and to exercise like Authority over all Places purchased by the Consent of the Legislature of the State in which the Same shall be, for the Erection of Forts, Magazines, Arsenals, Dockyards, and other needful Buildings;—And

To make all Laws which shall be necessary and proper for carrying into Execution the foregoing Powers, and all other Powers vested by this Constitution in the Government of the United States, or in any Department or Officer thereof.

Section 9. The Migration or Importation of such Persons as any of the States now existing shall think proper to admit, shall not be prohibited by the Congress prior to the Year one thousand eight hundred and eight, but a Tax or Duty may be imposed on such Importation, not exceeding ten dollars for each Person.

The Privilege of the Writ of Habeas Corpus shall not be suspended, unless when in Cases of Rebellion or Invasion the public Safety may require it.

No Bill of Attainder or ex post facto Law shall be passed.

No Capitation, or other direct, Tax shall be laid, unless in Proportion to the Census or Enumeration herein before directed to be taken.

No Tax or Duty shall be laid on Articles exported from any State.

No Preference shall be given by any Regulation of Commerce or Revenue to the Ports of one State over those of another: nor shall Vessels bound to, or from, one State, be obliged to enter, clear, or pay Duties in another.

No Money shall be drawn from the Treasury, but in Consequence of Appropriations made by Law; and a regular Statement and Account of the Receipts and Expenditures of all public Money shall be published from time to time.

No Title of Nobility shall be granted by the United States; and no Person holding any Office of Profit or Trust under them, shall, without the Consent of the Congress, accept of any present, Emolument, Office, or Title, of any kind whatever, from any King, Prince, or foreign State.

Section 10. No State shall enter into any Treaty, Alliance, or Confederation; grant Letters of Marque and Reprisal; coin Money; emit Bills of Credit; make any Thing but gold and silver Coin a Tender in Payment of Debts; pass any Bill of Attainder, ex post facto

Law, or Law impairing the Obligation of Contracts, or grant any Title of Nobility.

No State shall, without the Consent of the Congress, lay any Imposts or Duties on Imports or Exports, except what may be absolutely necessary for executing it's inspection Laws: and the net Produce of all Duties and Imposts, laid by any State on Imports or Exports, shall be for the Use of the Treasury of the United States; and all such Laws shall be subject to the Revision and Controul of the Congress.

No State shall, without the Consent of Congress, lay any Duty of Tonnage, keep Troops, or Ships of War in time of Peace, enter into any Agreement or Compact with another State, or with a foreign Power, or engage in War, unless actually invaded, or in such imminent Danger as will not admit of delay.

ARTICLE II.

Section 1. The executive Power shall be vested in a President of the United States of America. He shall hold his Office during the Term of four Years, and, together with the Vice President chosen for the same Term, be elected, as follows:

Each State shall appoint, in such Manner as the Legislature thereof may direct, a Number of Electors, equal to the whole Number of Senators and Representatives to which the State may be entitled in the Congress: but no Senator or Representative, or Person holding an Office of Trust or Profit under the United States, shall be appointed an Elector.

The Electors shall meet in their respective States, and vote by Ballot for two Persons, of whom one at least shall not be an Inhabitant of the same State with themselves. And they shall make a List of all the Persons voted for, and of the Number of Votes for each; which List they shall sign and certify, and transmit sealed to the Seat of the Government of the United States, directed to the President of the Senate. The President of the Senate shall, in the Presence of the Senate and House of Representatives, open all the Certificates, and the Votes shall then be counted.

The Person having the greatest Number of Votes shall be the President, if such Number be a Majority of the whole Number of Electors appointed; and if there be more than one who have such Majority, and have an equal Number of votes, then the House of Representatives shall immediately chuse by Ballot one of them for President; and if no Person have a Majority, then from the five highest on the List the said House shall in like Manner chuse the President. But in chusing the President,
the Votes shall be taken by States, the Representation from each State having one Vote; a Quorum for this Purpose shall consist of a Member or Members from two thirds of the States, and a Majority of all the States shall be necessary to a Choice. In every Case, after the Choice of the President, the Person having the greatest Number of Votes of the Electors shall be the Vice President. But if there should remain two or more who have equal Votes, the Senate shall chuse from them by Ballot the Vice President.

The Congress may determine the Time of chusing the Electors, and the Day on which they shall give their Votes; which Day shall be the same throughout the United States.

No Person except a natural born Citizen, or a Citizen of the United States, at the time of the Adoption of this Constitution, shall be eligible to the Office of President; neither shall any Person be eligible to that Office who shall not have attained to the Age of thirty five Years, and been fourteen Years a Resident within the United States.

In Case of the Removal of the President from Office, or of his Death, Resignation, or Inability to discharge the Powers and Duties of the said Office, the Same shall devolve on the Vice President, and the

Congress may by Law provide for the Case of Removal, Death, Resignation or Inability, both of the President and Vice President, declaring what Officer shall then act as President, and such Officer shall act accordingly, until the Disability be removed, or a President shall be elected.

The President shall, at stated Times, receive for his Services, a Compensation, which shall neither be encreased nor diminished during the Period for which he shall have been elected, and he shall not receive within that Period any other Emolument from the United States, or any of them.

Before he enter on the Execution of his Office, he shall take the following Oath or Affirmation:—"I do solemnly swear (or affirm) that I will faithfully execute the Office of President of the United States, and will to the best of my Ability, preserve, protect and defend the Constitution of the United States."

Section 2. The President shall be Commander in Chief of the Army and Navy of the United States, and of the Militia of the several States, when called into the actual Service of the United States; he may require the Opinion, in writing, of the principal officer in each of the executive Departments, upon any Subject relating to the Duties of their respective Offices, and he shall have Power to grant Reprieves and Pardons for Offenses against the United States, except in Cases of impeachment.

He shall have Power, by and with the Advice and Consent of the Senate, to make Treaties, provided two thirds of the Senators present concur; and he shall nominate, and by and with the Advice and Consent of the Senate, shall appoint Ambassadors, other public Ministers and Consuls, Judges of the supreme Court, and all other Officers of the United States, whose Appointments are not herein otherwise provided for, and which shall be established by Law: but the Congress may by Law vest the Appointment of such inferior

Officers, as they think proper, in the President alone, in the Courts of Law, or in the Heads of Departments.

The President shall have Power to fill up all Vacancies that may happen during the Recess of the Senate, by granting Commissions which shall expire at the End of their next session.

Section 3. He shall from time to time give to the Congress Information of the State of the Union, and recommend to their Consideration such Measures as he shall judge necessary and expedient; he may, on extraordinary Occasions, convene both Houses, or either of them, and in Case of Disagreement between them, with Respect to the Time of Adjournment, he may adjourn them to such Time as he shall think proper; he shall receive Ambassadors and other public Ministers; he shall take Care that the Laws be faithfully executed, and shall Commission all the Officers of the United States.

Section 4. The President, Vice President and all civil Officers of the United States, shall be removed from Office on Impeachment for, and Conviction of, Treason, Bribery, or other high Crimes and Misdemeanors.

ARTICLE III.

Section 1. The judicial Power of the United States, shall be vested in one supreme Court, and in such inferior Courts as the Congress may from time to time ordain and establish. The Judges, both of the supreme and inferior Courts, shall hold their Offices during good behavior, and shall, at stated Times, receive for their Services, a Compensation, which shall not be diminished during their Continuance in Office.

Section 2. The judicial Power shall extend to all Cases, in Law and Equity, arising under this Constitution, the Laws of the United States, and Treaties made, or which shall be made, under their Authority; to all Cases affecting Ambassadors, other public Ministers and Consuls; to all Cases of admiralty and maritime Jurisdiction; to Controversies to which the United States shall be a Party; to Controversies between two or more States; between a State and Citizens of another State; between Citizens of different States; between Citizens of the same State claiming Lands under Grants of different States, and between a State, or the Citizens thereof, and foreign States, Citizens or Subjects.

In all cases affecting Ambassadors, other public Ministers and Consuls, and those in which a State shall be Party, the supreme Court shall have original Jurisdiction. In all the other Cases before mentioned, the supreme Court shall have appellate Jurisdiction, both as to Law and Fact, with such Exceptions, and under such Regulations as the Congress shall make.

The Trial of all Crimes, except in Cases of Impeachment, shall be by Jury; and such Trial shall be held in the State where the said Crimes shall have been committed; but when not committed within any State, the Trial shall be at such Place or Places as the Congress may by Law have directed.

Section 3. Treason against the United States, shall consist only in levying War against them, or in adhering to their Enemies, giving them Aid and Comfort. No Person shall be convicted of Treason unless on the Testimony of two Witnesses to the same overt Act, or on Confession in open Court.

The Congress shall have power to declare the punishment of Treason, but no Attainder of Treason shall work Corruption of Blood, or Forfeiture except during the Life of the Person attainted.

ARTICLE IV.

Section 1. Full Faith and Credit shall be given in each State to the public Acts, Records, and judicial Proceedings of every other State.

And the Congress may by general Laws prescribe the Manner in which such Acts, Records, and Proceedings shall be proved, and the Effect thereof.

Section 2. The Citizens of each State shall be entitled to all Privileges and Immunities of Citizens in the several States.

A Person charged in any State with Treason, Felony, or other Crime, who shall flee from Justice, and be found in another State, shall on Demand of the executive Authority of the State from which he fled, be delivered up, to be removed to the State having Jurisdiction of the Crime.

No person held to Service or Labor in one State, under the Laws thereof, escaping into another, shall, in Consequence of any Law or Regulation therein, be discharged from such Service or Labor, But shall be delivered up on Claim of the Party to whom such Service or Labor may be due.

Section 3. New States may be admitted by the Congress into this Union; but no new States shall be formed or erected within the Jurisdiction of any other State; nor any State be formed by the Junction of two or more States, or Parts of States, without the Consent of the Legislatures of the States concerned as well as of the Congress.

The Congress shall have Power to dispose of and make all needful Rules and Regulations respecting the Territory or other Property belonging to the United States; and nothing in this Constitution shall be so construed as to Prejudice any Claims of the United States, or of any particular State.

Section 4. The United States shall guarantee to every State in this Union a Republican Form of Government, and shall protect each of them against Invasion; and on Application of the Legislature, or of the Executive (when the Legislature cannot be convened) against domestic Violence.

ARTICLE V.

The Congress, whenever two thirds of both Houses shall deem it necessary, shall propose Amendments to this Constitution, or, on the Application of the Legislatures of two thirds of the several States, shall call a Convention for proposing Amendments, which, in either Case, shall be valid to all Intents and Purposes, as Part of this Constitution, when ratified by the Legislatures of three fourths of the several States, or by Conventions in three fourths thereof, as the one or the other Mode of Ratification may be proposed by the Congress; Provided that no Amendment which may be made prior to the Year one thousand eight hundred and eight shall in any Manner affect the first and fourth Clauses in the ninth Section of the first Article; and that no State, without its Consent, shall be deprived of it's equal Suffrage in the Senate.

ARTICLE VI.

All Debts contracted and Engagements entered into, before the Adoption of this Constitution, shall be as valid against the United States under this Constitution, as under the Confederation.

This Constitution, and the Laws of the United States which shall be made in Pursuance thereof; and all Treaties made, or which shall be made, under the Authority of the United States, shall be the supreme Law of the Land; and the Judges in every State shall be bound thereby, any Thing in the Constitution or Laws of any State to the Contrary notwithstanding.

The Senators and Representatives before mentioned, and the Members of the several State Legislatures, and all executive and judicial Officers, both of the United States and of the several States, shall be bound by Oath or Affirmation, to support this Constitution; but no religious Test shall ever be required as a Qualification to any Office or public Trust under the United States

ARTICLE VII.

The Ratification of the Conventions of nine States, shall be sufficient for the Establishment of this Constitution between the States so ratifying the Same.

Done in Convention by the Unanimous Consent of the States present the Seventeenth Day of September in the Year of our Lord one thousand seven hundred and eighty seven and of the Independence of the United States of America the Twelfth. In Witness whereof We have hereunto subscribed our Names...

The Bill of Rights

The ratification of the new Constitution stood on extremely shaky ground in several of the States, until the common concerns for the rights of the sovereign People of America should be addressed. Having just won a very hard-fought war against the British crown, the American People were loath to allow a new central government take the place of the old monarchy and faraway Parliament.

Again, James Madison played a critical role, as in drafting the better part of the body of the Constitution, Madison drafted a Bill of Rights originally consisting of 12 Amendments, ten of which were ratified by the States and leading them to ratify the entire document. Madison's "Anti-pay-grab Amendment" was approved or supported by North Carolina, Virginia, New York, Massachussetts, Kentucky, and Tennessee over the 40 years following original ratification, but Madison's "12th Amendment" was finally ratified on May 5, 1992 – a full 203 years after Madison first wrote it.

Preamble

Congress of the United States begun and held at the <u>City of New York</u>, on Wednesday the fourth of March, one thousand seven hundred and eighty-nine.

The Conventions of a number of the States, having at the time of their <u>adopting</u> the Constitution expressed a desire in order to prevent misconstruction or abuse of its powers, that further declaratory and restrictive clauses should be added: And as extending the ground of public confidence in the Government will best ensure the beneficent ends of its institution.

Resolved by the Senate and House of Representatives of the United States of America in Congress assembled, two thirds of both Houses concurring that the following Articles be proposed to the Legislatures of the several states as Amendments to the Constitution of the United States, all or any of which articles, when ratified by three fourths of the said Legislatures to be valid to all intents and purposes as part of the said Constitution. viz.

Articles in addition to, and Amendment of the Constitution of the United States of America, proposed by Congress and Ratified by the Legislatures of the several States, pursuant to the fifth Article of the original Constitution.

AMENDMENT #1

Congress shall make no law respecting an establishment of religion, or prohibiting the free exercise thereof; or abridging the freedom of speech, or of the press; or the right of the people peaceably to assemble, and to petition the Government for a redress of grievances.

AMENDMENT #2

A well regulated Militia, being necessary to the security of a free State, the right of the people to keep and bear Arms, shall not be infringed.

AMENDMENT #3

No Soldier shall, in time of peace be quartered in any house, without the consent of the Owner, nor in time of war, but in a manner to be prescribed by law.

AMENDMENT #4

The right of the people to be secure in their persons, houses, papers, and effects, against unreasonable searches and seizures, shall not be violated, and no Warrants shall issue, but upon probable cause, supported by Oath or affirmation, and particularly describing the place to be searched, and the persons or things to be seized.

AMENDMENT #5

No person shall be held to answer for a capital, or otherwise infamous crime, unless on a presentment or indictment of a Grand Jury, except in cases arising in the land or naval forces, or in the Militia, when in actual service in time of War or public danger; nor shall any person be subject for the same offence to be twice put in jeopardy of life or limb; nor shall be compelled in any criminal case to be a witness against himself, nor be deprived of life, liberty, or property, without due process of law; nor shall private property be taken for public use, without just compensation.

AMENDMENT #6

In all criminal prosecutions, the accused shall enjoy the right to a speedy and public trial, by an impartial jury of the State and district wherein the crime shall have been committed, which district shall have been previously ascertained by law, and to be informed of the nature and cause of the accusation; to be confronted with the witnesses against him; to have compulsory process for obtaining witnesses in his favor, and to have the Assistance of Counsel for his defence.

AMENDMENT #7

In Suits at common law, where the value in controversy shall exceed twenty dollars, the right of trial by jury shall be preserved, and no fact tried by a jury, shall be otherwise re-examined in any Court of the United States, than according to the rules of the common law.

AMENDMENT #8

Excessive bail shall not be required, nor excessive fines imposed, nor cruel and unusual punishments inflicted.

AMENDMENT #9

The enumeration in the Constitution of certain rights, shall not be construed to deny or disparage others retained by the people.

AMENDMENT #10

The powers not delegated to the United States by the Constitution, nor prohibited by it to the States, are reserved to the States respectively, or to the people.

AMENDMENT #11

The Judicial power of the United States shall not be construed to extend to any suit in law or equity, commenced or prosecuted against one of the United States by Citizens of another State, or by Citizens or Subjects of any Foreign State.

AMENDMENT #12

The Electors shall meet in their respective states, and vote by ballot for President and Vice-President, one of whom, at least, shall not be an inhabitant of the same state with themselves; they shall name in their ballots the person voted for as President, and in distinct ballots the person voted for as Vice-President, and they shall make distinct lists of all persons voted for as President, and of all persons voted for as Vice-President, and of the number of votes for each, which lists they shall sign and certify, and transmit sealed to the seat of the government of the United States, directed to the President of the Senate;—The President of the Senate shall, in the presence of the Senate and House of Representatives, open all the certificates and the votes shall then be counted; The person having the greatest number of votes for President, shall be the President, if such number be a majority of the whole number of Electors appointed; and if no person have such majority, then from the persons having the highest numbers not exceeding three on the list of those voted for as President, the House of Representatives shall choose immediately, by ballot, the President. But in choosing the President, the votes shall be taken by states, the representation from each state having one vote; a quorum for this purpose shall consist of a member or members from two-thirds of the states, and a majority of all the states shall be necessary to a choice. And if the House of Representatives shall not choose a President whenever the right of choice shall devolve upon them, before the fourth day of March next following, then the Vice-President shall act as President, as in the case of the death or other constitutional disability of the President.

The person having the greatest number of votes as Vice-President, shall be the Vice-President, if such number be a majority of the whole number of Electors appointed, and if no person have a majority, then from the two highest numbers on the list, the Senate shall choose the Vice-President; a quorum for the purpose shall consist of two-thirds of the whole number of Senators, and a majority of the whole number shall be necessary to a choice. But no person constitutionally ineligible to the office of President shall be eligible to that of Vice-President of the United States.

AMENDMENT #13

Neither slavery nor involuntary servitude, except as a punishment for crime whereof the party shall have been duly convicted, shall exist within the United States, or any place subject to their jurisdiction. Congress shall have power to enforce this article by appropriate legislation.

AMENDMENT #14

Section 1. All persons born or naturalized in the United States, and subject to the jurisdiction thereof, are citizens of the United States and of the State wherein they reside. No State shall make or enforce any law which shall abridge the privileges or immunities of citizens of the United States; nor shall any State deprive any person of life, liberty, or property, without due process of law; nor deny to any person within its jurisdiction the equal protection of the laws.

Section 2. Representatives shall be apportioned among the several States according to their respective numbers, counting the whole number of persons in each State, excluding Indians not taxed. But when the right to vote at any election for the choice of electors for President and Vice President of the United States, Representatives in Congress, the Executive and Judicial officers of a State, or the members of the Legislature thereof, is denied to any of the male inhabitants of such State, being twenty-one years of age, and citizens of the United States, or in any way abridged, except for participation in rebellion, or other crime, the basis of representation therein shall be reduced in the proportion which the number of such male citizens shall bear to the whole number of male citizens twenty-one years of age in such State.

Section 3. No person shall be a Senator or Representative in Congress, or elector of President and Vice President, or hold any office, civil or military, under the United States, or under any State, who, having previously taken an oath, as a member of Congress, or as an officer of the United States, or as a member of any State legislature, or as an executive or judicial officer of any State, to support the Constitution of the United States, shall have engaged in insurrection or rebellion against the same, or given aid or comfort to the enemies thereof. But Congress may by a vote of two-thirds of each House, remove such disability.

Section 4. The validity of the public debt of the United States, authorized by law, including debts incurred for payment of pensions and bounties for services in suppressing insurrection or rebellion, shall not be questioned. But neither the United States nor any State shall assume or pay any debt or obligation incurred in aid of insurrection or rebellion against the United States, or any claim for the loss or emancipation of any slave; but all such debts, obligations and claims shall be held illegal and void.

Section 5. The Congress shall have power to enforce, by appropriate legislation, the provisions of this article.

AMENDMENT #15

The right of citizens of the United States to vote shall not be denied or abridged by the United States or by any State on account of race, color, or previous condition of servitude. The Congress shall have power to enforce this article by appropriate legislation.

AMENDMENT #16

The Congress shall have power to lay and collect taxes on incomes, from whatever source derived, without apportionment among the several States, and without regard to any census or enumeration.

AMENDMENT #17

The Senate of the United States shall be composed of two Senators from each State, elected by the people thereof, for six years; and each Senator shall have one vote. The electors in each State shall have the qualifications requisite for electors of the most numerous branch of the State legislatures.

When vacancies happen in the representation of any State in the Senate, the executive authority of such State shall issue writs of election to fill such vacancies: Provided, That the legislature of any State may empower the executive thereof to make temporary appointments until the people fill the vacancies by election as the legislature may direct. This amendment shall not be so construed as to affect the election or term of any Senator chosen before it becomes valid as part of the Constitution.

AMENDMENT #18

Section 1. After one year from the ratification of this article the manufacture, sale, or transportation of intoxicating liquors within, the importation thereof into, or the exportation thereof from the United States and all territory subject to the jurisdiction thereof for beverage purposes is hereby prohibited.

Section 2. The Congress and the several States shall have concurrent power to enforce this article by appropriate legislation.

Section 3. This article shall be inoperative unless it shall have been ratified as an amendment to the Constitution by the legislatures of the several States, as provided in the Constitution, within seven years from the date of the submission hereof to the States by the Congress.

AMENDMENT #19

The right of citizens of the United States to vote shall not be denied or abridged by the United States or by any State on account of sex. Congress shall have power to enforce this article by appropriate legislation.

AMENDMENT #20

Section 1. The terms of the President and Vice President shall end at noon on the 20th day of January, and the terms of Senators and Representatives at noon on the 3d day of January, of the years in which such terms would have ended if this article had not been ratified; and the terms of their successors shall then begin.
Section 2. The Congress shall assemble at least once in every year, and such meeting shall begin at noon on the 3d day of January, unless they shall by law appoint a different day. ^{affects 5}

Section 3. If, at the time fixed for the beginning of the term of the President, the President elect shall have died, the Vice President elect shall become President. If a President shall not have been chosen before the time fixed for the beginning of his term, or if the President elect shall have failed to qualify, then the Vice President elect shall act as President until a President shall have qualified; and the Congress may by law provide for the case wherein neither a President elect nor a Vice President elect shall have qualified, declaring who shall then act as President, or the manner in which one who is to act shall be selected, and such person shall act accordingly until a President or Vice President shall have qualified.

Section 4. The Congress may by law provide for the case of the death of any of the persons from whom the House of Representatives may choose a President whenever the right of choice shall have devolved upon them, and for the case of the death of any of the persons from whom the Senate may choose a Vice President whenever the right of choice shall have devolved upon them.

Section 5. Sections 1 and 2 shall take effect on the 15th day of October following the ratification of this article.

Section 6. This article shall be inoperative unless it shall have been ratified as an amendment to the Constitution by the legislatures of three-fourths of the several States within seven years from the date of its submission.

AMENDMENT #21

Section 1. The eighteenth article of amendment to the Constitution of the United States is hereby repealed.

Section 2. The transportation or importation into any State, Territory, or possession of the United States for delivery or use therein of intoxicating liquors, in violation of the laws thereof, is hereby prohibited.

Section 3. This article shall be inoperative unless it shall have been ratified as an amendment to the Constitution by conventions in the several States, as provided in the Constitution, within seven years from the date of the submission hereof to the States by the Congress.

AMENDMENT #22

Section 1. No person shall be elected to the office of the President more than twice, and no person who has held the office of President, or acted as President, for more than two years of a term to which some other person was elected President shall be elected to the office of the President more than once. But this article shall not apply to any person holding the office of President when this article was proposed by the Congress, and shall not prevent any person who may be holding the office of President, or acting as President, during the term within which this article becomes operative from holding the office of President or acting as President during the remainder of such term.

Section 2. This article shall be inoperative unless it shall have been ratified as an amendment to the Constitution by the legislatures of three-fourths of the several states within seven years from the date of its submission to the states by the Congress.

AMENDMENT #23

Section 1. The District constituting the seat of government of the United States shall appoint in such manner as the Congress may direct: A number of electors of President and Vice President equal to the whole number of Senators and Representatives in Congress to which the District would be entitled if it were a state, but in no event more than the least populous state; they shall be in addition to those appointed by the states, but they shall be considered, for the purposes of the election of President and Vice President, to be electors appointed by a state; and they shall meet in the District and perform such duties as provided by the twelfth article of amendment.

Section 2. The Congress shall have power to enforce this article by appropriate legislation.

AMENDMENT #24

Section 1. The right of citizens of the United States to vote in any primary or other election for President or Vice President, for electors for President or Vice President, or for Senator or Representative in Congress, shall not be denied or abridged by the United States or any state by reason of failure to pay any poll tax or other tax.

Section 2. The Congress shall have power to enforce this article by appropriate legislation.

AMENDMENT #25

Section 1. In case of the removal of the President from office or of his death or resignation, the Vice President shall become President.

Section 2. Whenever there is a vacancy in the office of the Vice President, the President shall nominate a Vice President who shall take office upon confirmation by a majority vote of both Houses of Congress.

Section 3. Whenever the President transmits to the President pro tempore of the Senate and the Speaker of the House of Representatives his written declaration that he is unable to discharge the powers and duties of his office, and until he transmits to them a written declaration to the contrary, such powers and duties shall be discharged by the Vice President as Acting President.

Section 4. Whenever the Vice President and a majority of either the principal officers of the executive departments or of such other body as Congress may by law provide, transmit to the President pro tempore of the Senate and the Speaker of the House of Representatives their written declaration that the President is unable to discharge the powers and duties of his office, the Vice President shall immediately assume the powers and duties of the office as Acting President.

Thereafter, when the President transmits to the President pro tempore of the Senate and the Speaker of the House of Representatives his written declaration that no inability exists, he shall resume the powers and duties of his office unless the Vice President and a majority of either the principal officers of the executive department or of such other body as Congress may by law provide, transmit within four days to the President pro tempore of the Senate and the Speaker of the House of Representatives their written declaration that the President is unable to discharge the powers and duties of his office. Thereupon Congress shall decide the issue, assembling within forty-eight hours for that purpose if not in session. If the Congress, within twenty-one days after receipt of the latter written declaration, or, if Congress is not in session, within twenty-one days after Congress is required to assemble, determines by two-thirds vote of both Houses that the President is unable to discharge the powers and duties of his office, the Vice President shall continue to discharge the same as Acting President; otherwise, the President shall resume the powers and duties of his office.

AMENDMENT #26

Section 1. The right of citizens of the United States, who are 18 years of age or older, to vote, shall not be denied or abridged by the United States or any state on account of age.

2: The Congress shall have the power to enforce this article by appropriate legislation.

AMENDMENT #27

No law varying the compensation for the services of the Senators and Representatives shall take effect until an election of Representatives shall have intervened.

Appendix C:

The AmericaAgain! Declaration

We the People of these united States declare that our Republic was founded as a union of sovereign States; that the compact ratified by twelve States in 1788 remains the entire grant of powers that We the People allowed to national government; That a solemn regard for the natural rights of Life, Liberty and Private Property granted by Our Creator demands that we remind our civil governments that no man acting with consent of another can remove these God-given rights as they have done; That ancestry and posterity compel us as free citizens of these sovereign States to secure these rights, to begin enforcing our national compact before a watching world; thus do We, the People of these United States, declare that:

1. We the People of the 50 sovereign States were the creators of the Constitution for the united States of America.

2. The three branches of federal government are creatures — things created by us – in the U.S. Constitution.

3. The national Constitution is the highest and most basic Law of the Land throughout this Republic so uniquely blessed by God among all nations.

4. The duty to preserve, protect, and defend the Constitution for the united States of America is the duty of *every American citizen.* This includes all members of Congress and sovereign State legislatures; all U.S. presidents and governors of the sovereign States; all judges whether State or federal; all armed forces whether under State or federal leaders, mustered formally or informally, active or veteran; and all peace officers whether police, constable, sheriff, highway patrol, or Texas Ranger.

5. In the Constitution, We the People clearly enumerated and limited the powers of the federal government and retained any powers not specifically enumerated therein, to ourselves and our sovereign States.

6. Any exercise of power by federal government beyond those listed powers is and has been a violation of the Supreme Law of the Land.

7. President Jefferson said that "in questions of powers...let no more be heard of confidence in man, but bind him down from mischief by the chains of the Constitution".

8. Such "binding down" can be peaceably effected by binding the federal purse and by We the People and Sovereign States enforcing that Law of Limitation for the first time in the history of our Constitution.

9. The present $3,700,000,000,000 annual federal revenue has spawned a brood of corruptions as unlimited sums of money always do, the ocean of D.C. cash now funding unconstitutional federal powers, cabinet departments, agents, agencies, programs, projects, offices, and regulations that for sheer number are impossible to list here, but that threaten our livelihoods, liberties, property, and posterity, making a standing joke of our Law of the Land; and fair game out of the people of foreign lands.

10. Thomas Jefferson also wrote in the Kentucky Resolution that, *"the several States composing the United States of America, are not united on the principles of unlimited submission to their General Government; but that by compact under the style and title of a Constitution for the united States and of amendments thereto, they constituted a general government for special purposes, delegated to that government certain definite powers, reserving each State to itself, the residuary mass of right to their own self Government; and that whensoever the general government assumes undelegated powers, its acts are unauthoritative, void, and of no force: That to this compact each State acceded as a State, and is an integral party, its co-States forming as to itself, the other party: That the government created by this compact was not made the exclusive or final judge of the extent of the powers delegated to itself, since that would have made its discretion and not the Constitution, the measure of its powers; but that as in all other cases of compact among parties having no common Judge, each party [sovereign State] has an equal right to judge of itself, as well of infractions as of the mode and measure of redress.";*

11. James Madison concurred, saying that *"The States, then, being the parties to the constitutional compact, and in their sovereign capacity, it follows of necessity that there can be no tribunal above their authority to decide...whether the compact made by them be violated; and consequently that as the parties to it, they must themselves decide...such questions as may be of sufficient magnitude to require their interposition."*

12. In Federalist #28, Alexander Hamilton asserted the obvious right of We the People to constrain federal tyranny, saying that *"The whole power of the proposed government is to be in the hands of the representatives of the People. This is the essential and, after all, only efficacious security for the rights and privileges of the People... (I)f the representatives of the People betray their constituents, there is no resource left but...self-defense...".*

13. Hamilton reminded citizens that as long as we understand basic civics, exercising our power as creators of the federal government, we can prevail: *"the larger the American population would become, the more effectively we can resist federal government tyranny... The obstacles to usurpation and the facilities of resistance increase with the increased extent of the (body of citizens), provided the citizens understand their rights and are disposed to defend them. The natural strength of the people in a large community, in proportion to the artificial size of the government, is greater than in a small...".*

14. Although a proponent of strong federal government, even Mr. Hamilton recognised the danger of wayward or tyrannical State or national government, making it clear that the sovereign People would be the deciding factor in either case, saying, *"Power being almost always the rival of power, the general government will at all times stand ready to check the usurpations of State governments, and these will have the same disposition towards the general government. The People, by throwing themselves into either scale, will infallibly make it preponderate. If their rights are invaded by either, they can make use of the other as the instrument of redress... The State governments will...afford complete security against invasions of the public liberty by the national authority...possessing all the organs of civil power, and the confidence of the People, they can at once adopt a regular plan of opposition, in which they can combine all the resources of the community. They can readily communicate with each other in the different States, and unite their common forces for the protection of their common liberty.".*

15. The mission of AmericaAgain! is to make good on the guarantees offered in the Federalist Papers to our forefathers, in order to entice them to ratify the Constitution.

16. All three branches of our federal creature have ceased to check-and-balance one another, instead colluding over the past 150 years abusing the "necessary and proper" and "general welfare"

clauses to fashion a lawless, limitless system of power, pork, and perquisites warned against by James Madison, the primary author of the Constitution: *"…it is evident that there is not a single power whatever, which may not have some reference to the common defense or the general welfare; nor a power of any magnitude which, in its exercise, does not involve or admit an application of money. The government, therefore, which possesses power in either one or other of these extents, is a government without the limitations formed by a particular enumeration of powers. Consequently, the meaning and effect of this particular enumeration is destroyed by the exposition given to these general phrases…Congress is authorized to provide money for the common defense and general welfare. In both, is subjoined to this authority an enumeration of the cases to which their power shall extend…a question arises whether (any) particular measure be within the enumerated authorities vested in Congress. If it be, the money requisite for it may be applied to it; if it be not, no such application can be made."; "It is incumbent in this, as in every other exercise of power by the federal government, to prove from the Constitution, that it grants the particular power exercised."*.

17. Congress and presidents for many generations have violated the highest law in America in precisely this way, at a cost of tens of trillions of dollars, and the further cost of our liberty, privacy, and rights to property and peaceful self-government.

18. When a government of, by, and for The People stands in perennial, collusive violation of the Constitution, We The People have constitutional authority to take enforcement action on our own initiative in a peaceful, lawful manner.

19. The duty of constitutional law enforcement falls on We the People, not by resisting government's lawlessness with a lawlessness of our own but rather through having the courts of our sovereign States bring law enforcement power to bear as our right and duty under that Law.

20. All aspirants to Congress implicitly represent to the voters that they understand the Constitution and will enforce it once elected. Upon entering office, they take an oath stating, *"I do solemnly swear (or affirm) that I will support and defend the Constitution of the United States...that I will bear true faith and allegiance to the same...",* by which oath the Constitution requires that they shall be bound.

21. The president of the United States takes the oath that he *"will to the best of my ability, preserve, protect and defend the Constitution",* with the Constitution imposing upon him the duty that *"he shall take Care that the Laws be faithfully executed",* including his own oath of office; and any willful violation of any such oath through treaty, executive order, or exercise of imperial powers is an act of usurpation, tyranny, or both, as well as a violation of every American's right to a constitutionally legitimate government based upon the consent of the governed.

22. With respect to compliance with his "Oath or Affirmation, to support this Constitution", no public official can ever be allowed to be the judge of his own case, as Presidents Jefferson and Madison observed.

23. The nefarious practice of 'executive orders' is nowhere authorized in Article II of the Constitution. Numerous such executive fiats are demonstrable violations of the limited powers stipulated in Article II, yet We The People have had no voice in said imperial edicts issued by presidents.

24. The same principle holds true for treaties signed by tyrannical presidents under the noses of the American people, and to our clear detriment yet without sufficient popular review before being trundled through a complicit U.S. Senate.

25. We the People "ordained and established" the Constitution; a fundamental principle of law is that the power to enact carries with it the final authority to declare the meaning of legislation.

26. Every public official's oath is made to We the People; the Constitution commands that the official be bound by that oath; thus We the People have the right to enforce that oath and the power to do so as well, for no right can exist without an effective remedy, including remedy via State courts.

27. Congressman Henry Hyde, Chairman of the House International Relations Committee, responding to Congressman Ron Paul's defense of the Constitution's war powers clauses and opposing George W. Bush's Iraq Resolution in 2002, made the treasonous assertion apparently shared by most of Congress and a succession of presidents, asserting that *"there are things in the Constitution that have been overtaken by events, by time...things that are no longer relevant to a modern society...things that are inappropriate, anachronistic".*

28. We the People have seen that reform legislation never proceeds through the halls of the corrupted Congress, but is invariably negotiated away by co-conspirators therein; that the corrupt practices of Congress have now infested our State, county, and municipal governments also, as the U.S. Supreme Court suggested in its 1928 Olmsted ruling: *"In a government of laws... Our government is the potent, the omnipresent teacher. For good or for ill, it teaches the whole people by its example. Crime is contagious. If the government becomes a lawbreaker, it breeds contempt for law...".*

29. Congress has perennially refused to balance its federal budgets.

30. The flow of illegal aliens across our borders reached epidemic proportions long ago, yet Congress refuses to seal the borders,

instead playing political games with a ticking time bomb against our culture, economy, and civil order; saddling Taxpayers with the cost of socialist programs for illegal aliens, the politicians' future political pawns. America was always a melting pot Republic with a common language, currency, culture and work ethic, in one generation it has become a polyglot of warring factions seeking an African America or Mexican America.

31. The U.S. House of Representatives and U.S. Senate were intended to be populated by citizen-statesmen for limited terms so that no lifelong political oligarchy would rise up to rule over the 'common people' as is now the case, with members of Congress being wealthy, insular individuals with little affinity with, or empathy for, the average citizen.

32. Members of Congress are in the habit of decrying the opulent lives of corporate CEOs, while shamelessly enjoying the very same opulence – fat pensions, paid insurance premiums, free private spas, limousines, hundreds of millions in new private jets hidden in federal budgets…and much more – all paid for by citizens who will never enjoy such free luxuries ourselves.

33. The U.S. Congress is explicitly granted the sole authority to declare War and to "make Rules for the Government and Regulation of the land and naval forces" (Article 1, Section 8), and to control the funding of those same forces, but has heretofore lacked the fortitude to cut off funding for the undeclared, unprovoked foreign attacks and invasions by federal forces ordered by our presidents on pretenses that have often proven false.

34. There will always be men in the world whose goal is plunder, to amass insane wealth; such chieftains buy and trade politicians as game pieces, world without end. Whenever such men in the name of their military machines, their nations, their family or

corporate interests seek empire over or to attack the American mainland, citizens, or infrastructure on that mainland, this is reason for military and intelligence countermeasures authorized by the U.S. Congress.

35. However, when our federal government projects military power across the globe on behalf of such private and corporate interests, not in defense of our own mainland or citizens and infrastructure therein, there exists no constitutional or moral authority for U.S. military involvement.

36. It is illegal, immoral, and un-American for the U.S. military to plunder foreign resources and threaten foreign peoples who present no threat to us, promulgating the propaganda that the armed forces are "establishing democracy". Unless We the People of the sovereign States should vote for any such exploit, it cannot possibly be democratic, and no democracy is created via armed invasion.

37. We the People demand accountability, transparency, integrity, and rule of law to restrain such lawlessness by Congress and our presidents on behalf of those who seek empire over the world. If the only difference that the United States military brings to conquered lands is corporate logos to replace Arab family crests on storage tanks, wellhead equipment, and mine shaft entrances – we citizens and sovereign States of America will continue to be seen needlessly as enemies.

38. The vast majority of the American people were once Christian, and most Americans profess Christianity at least in name. The melting-pot American culture that made us the envy of the world was the ethic of Christ, not that of Judaism or Islam.

39. Under our Constitution it is illegal for Congress to grant a concession for manufacture of our currency to a private banking

cartel to which We the People are forced to pay the face value plus interest on illegal, worthless paper currency.

40. Congress has willfully and knowingly allowed the Internal Revenue Service to perennially violate the federal tax laws, regulations, and its own operating manual, transforming Taxpayers by coercion into pack-mules to carry the financial burdens of their demonstrable crimes and those of the industries who buy their allegiance, and using this tax agency as a terror organization to take retribution on political enemies and insure citizen compliance with immoral,, unconstitutional acts of Congress.

41. Every member of Congress and three successive administrations were hand-delivered packages of evidence that IRS is violating laws while calling its actions 'Code enforcement' – a shameless breach of public trust corroborated by the Historian of the IRS testifying before the U.S. Senate in 1997, and by a former IRS fraud examiner, former IRS attorney, former IRS-CID agent, two former IRS field agents, a former IRS auditor, and a former IRS Commissioner.

42. We refuse to allow Congress to burden future generations with an equally corrupt revenue-neutral 'fair' tax, so-called, that would continue to amass over four times the revenues required to fund enumerated federal powers. We will instead demand that as Tax Honesty grows from today's estimated 67 million non-filers to become the productive sector's majority view, that members of Congress accept these reduced revenues as Washington D.C.'s limits of power, as enumerated in the law.

43. The Second Amendment declares, *"A well regulated Militia, being necessary to the security of a free State, the right of the people to keep and bear Arms, shall not be infringed"*, and this is the only place in the Constitution where the term *security* appears. The

amendment inextricably links *security* with a free State, with no place for a para-militarized police state in America;

44. The obvious intent of the Second Amendment is for the People to exercise our right to keep and bear Arms, to provide our own security in our own States through our own well-regulated Militia. Since Congress has long refused to *"provide for organizing, arming, and disciplining, the Militia"*, as the Constitution requires in Article I, Section 8, Clause 16, We the People must organize and mobilize ourselves to restore well-regulated Militia in every State according to constitutional principles, through State legislation. However, modern reality as opposed to life in colonial times demands that prior and in addition to re-establishing the 'homeland security' of constitutional militias, We the People will use *unarmed* law enforcement.

After our long failure to perform our citizen duties, bearing the cost of our abdication on every hand, We the People of these fifty united States intend to lawfully, peacefully begin enforcing the Constitution in each of the 435 U.S. House districts and in each of our 50 States against its violation by our U.S. congressman and senators, effecting such law enforcement through local AmericaAgain! chapters singly and statewide.

We the People do hereby demand that those we elected and sent to serve us in the U.S. House of Representatives and the U.S. Senate:

1) Publicly reiterate Congress' intention to exercise Subsection (c) of the War Powers Resolution of 1973 without delay in any instance when an administration has initiated foreign hostilities or mobilized the U.S. military without a Declaration of War by Congress, and is unable to prove to Congress beyond reasonable doubt that such mobilization or hostilities are necessary to address a demonstrable threat to We the People and/or our sovereign States;

2) Enact legislation that:

    (a) Acknowledges the 4th Amendment privacy in the American people's own persons, houses, papers, email communications, vehicles and effects from any and all government surveillance, seizure, or detainment unless preceded by issuance of a specific, bona fide warrant issued on probable cause;

    (b) Repeals any and all portions of the FISA, RFPA, USA Patriot Act, and the Intelligence Authorization Act of 2004 that violate the 1st and 4th Amendment constitutional rights or the liberty and privacy of any American citizen;

    (c) Makes illegal any optical, electronic, or satellite surveillance, tracing, or tracking of any American citizen or that citizen's property until a *judicial* warrant is issued upon probable cause, supported by oath or affirmation and particularly describing the place, items, or electronic files to be searched and the persons or things to be seized;

    (d) Makes illegal any biometric tracking of any law-abiding citizen of these 50 States, or any federal government program of biometric or electronic tracking of domestic animals within any State;

3) Declares that neither Congress nor any president, nor any federal court, has the power to conscript Americans of any age or condition into involuntary 'national service' or servitude of any kind, for any purpose;

4) Enact a *Lawful American Currency and Banking Act* for at least the following purposes:

    (a) Declaring that We the People have delegated the power to 'coin Money' only to Congress, and have delegated to Congress only the power to 'coin Money', and that Congress lacks any authority to delegate or to fail, neglect, or refuse to exercise this power;

    (b) Declaring that the Federal Reserve Act of 1913, and all subsequent amendments of that act, are unconstitutional, and have been since their purported enactment, and that the special privileges that now attach to Federal Reserve Notes—to wit, that such notes shall be redeemed in lawful money by the United States Department of the Treasury, shall be receivable for all taxes and other public dues, and shall be legal tender for all debts, public and private—are unconstitutional, and have been since their purported enactment;

(c) As remedies for these violations of the Constitution, establishing as an alternative to the Federal Reserve System and Federal Reserve Notes, a system of official money consisting solely of gold and silver with gold to be the sole monetary peg with silver left to float at market rather than being pegged at a fixed ratio to gold, so as to avoid the timeless problem of bad money driving out good. Gold coins shall be valued in 'dollars' at the prevailing exchange rate between silver and gold in the free market. The alternative money to be produced through immediate free coinage of whatever gold and silver may be brought to the United States Mints and substituted for Federal Reserve Notes as rapidly as maintenance of stability throughout America's economy will permit, in all financial transactions of the general government. Congress shall so amend the Federal Reserve Act of 1913 (as amended) that after the effective date of such legislation, the Federal Reserve System shall have no official relationship whatsoever to the general government; Federal Reserve regional banks shall obtain new charters from the States consistent with the laws thereof, or shall cease doing business as of the date on which the Secretary of the Treasury shall certify that all financial transactions of the general government are being conducted solely in gold and silver;

(d) Acknowledging that the States have always enjoyed the right as sovereign governments and a duty pursuant to Article I, Section 10 of the Constitution to employ gold and silver coin to the exclusion of any other currency as their medium of exchange in their sovereign functions; that neither Congress, nor the president, nor any court of the general government or of the States, nor any international or supra-national body, nor any private parties have any authority whatsoever to require the States to employ anything other than gold and silver coin for such purposes;

(e) Making illegal the practice of 'fractional reserve banking', requiring that if any bank or financial institution that accepts deposits in the normal course of business shall be unable to pay all such deposits on demand, then the directors, officers, shareholders, partners, trustees, or other owners and managers (as the case may be) of such bank or financial institution shall be personally liable and their own personal assets subject to seizure to satisfy such unpaid deposit balances under the laws of the State in which the demand for payment of such balances is made; and

(f) Declaring null and void and imposing criminal penalties and civil damages on any person who purports to enact or enforce any purported tax or financial burden purportedly imposed on any exchange of one form of United States money for another form of money thereof, notwithstanding that the nominal value of one form may be different than the nominal value of the other form involved in the transaction. Such legislation shall apply to Federal Reserve Notes, base-metallic and debased silver coinage, and all paper currencies of the United States until the date on which the Secretary of the Treasury shall certify that all financial transactions of the general government are being conducted solely in gold and silver; thereafter only as Congress shall determine necessary.

5) Repeal the 16th Amendment; enact a constitutional amendment barring Congress from taxing personal wages and salaries; until such an amendment is ratified, enact interim legislation demanding that the Internal Revenue Service obey the Tax Code, cease all fraudulent application thereof, and exonerate all political

prisoners being held on 'failure to file' or similar unsubstantiated charges.

6) Repeal the 17th Amendment and enact an Amendment restoring the original plan of federalism in Article I, Section 3 of the Constitution: election of U.S. senators by their State Legislature except that a mere plurality shall be required, rather than a majority vote to win said election, thus restoring the original design of the U.S. Senate as representing the sovereign States, to check rash actions by the U.S. House and/or unconstitutional treaties and orders by presidents.

7) Enact legislation declaring that the federal government lacks constitutional authority to:

   (a) seize by purported eminent domain any private land, water, timber, oil, gas, minerals, or other natural resources in, on, or under such land in any State for any reason, under any conditions; or

   (b) purchase any private land, water, timber, oil, gas, minerals, or other natural resources in, on, or under such land in any State without the *"Consent of the Legislature of the State in which the Same shall be"*; and on the basis of such declarations, repealing or otherwise invalidating all "land-use regulations" and like federal controls, restrictions, and prohibitions that deprive private owners of the full use and enjoyment of their properties pursuant to the laws of the several States.

8) Enact legislation pursuant to Congress's power to *"provide for ... arming ... the Militia"* in Article I, Section 8, Clause 16 of the Constitution to repeal every statute, administrative regulation, executive order, or other directive with the purported force of law of federal government, and to preëmpt every such measure, present and future, of any State or subdivision thereof, that infringes on or burdens the right of any citizen of or legal resident alien in any State who is eligible for membership in that State's

Militia to purchase, own, possess, transport, or sell, whether inter-state or intrastate, any firearm, ammunition, or related accoutrements suitable for service in a "Militia" as that term is used in the Constitution for the united States; penalizes any individual for his or her use of a firearm in self-defense of himself, herself, or any other individual; infringes on or burdens, except on the same terms as apply to any other business, the right of any person to engage in the commercial design, manufacture, repair, sale and distribution, or other trade or occupation of or involving firearms, ammunition, and related accoutrements.

9) De-fund and dismantle the U.S. Department of Education and any federal funding passed on to States and thus supporting failed government education monopoly. We never granted government the power to program American minds with false versions of history, economics, and morality.

10) Enact an Amendment to the Constitution requiring all federal budgets presented to the president be balanced.

11) Enact legislation declaring English the official language of government in the USA and incorporate Senate Joint Resolution 6 of the 111th Congress, to end the illegal alien 'anchor baby' practice.

12) Enact legislation to begin securing our borders including existing citizens' plans to timely construct the U.S.-Mexico border fence with reasonable alternatives for the riverine sections of that border; environmental, regulatory, and bureaucratic requirements waived so that project(s) avoid the exorbitant time- and cost overruns common to government projects.

13) To avoid the dual legal systems seen today in nations such as the UK and Australia with respect to polygamy and other Muslim vagaries, enact legislation outlawing any aspect of Muslim

law (Shar'ia) which violates any local ordinance, State statute, federal statute, or any section of the U.S. Constitution or the Constitution of any of the 50 sovereign States of America.

14) Enact the *American Sovereignty Restoration Act of 2009* (H.R. 1146) of the first session of the 111th Congress, ending U.S. membership in the United Nations within 24 months, repealing various laws pertaining to the U.N., terminating the authorization of funds to be spent on the U.N., terminating U.N. presence on American soil, and withdrawing diplomatic immunity for U.N. employees.

15) Enact an amendment to the Constitution assuring the sovereignty of the American people and our sovereign States, which shall read:

Section 1. No provision of a treaty or international agreement conflicting with this Constitution, or not made in pursuance thereof, shall be the supreme Law of the Land nor shall it be of any force or effect.

Section 2. No provision of a treaty or other international agreement shall become effective as internal law in the United States until it is enacted through legislation in Congress acting within its constitutionally enumerated powers.

Section 3. Any vote regarding advising and consenting to ratification of a treaty shall be determined by yeas and nays, and the names of the persons voting for and against shall be entered in the Journal of the Senate.

16) Enact an amendment to the Constitution limiting terms for all members of Congress to two (2); abolishing congressional pensions retroactive and future (i.e., for every incumbent and retired member of Congress) and abolishing all *publicly-supported* congressional perquisites including but not limited to meals, lim-

ousines, charter aircraft, hairdressers, fitness memberships, spas, and health or life insurance premiums.

17) Enact legislation imposing criminal penalties on any individual or group within the federal government who unilaterally or with other individuals, transnational groups, organizations or foreign governments, attempts to compromise the legal or financial sovereignty of any or all of the 50 sovereign States of America or the sovereign citizens thereof, without the specific knowledge and consent of the legislature of each and every State whose citizens would be affected, regardless whether such action formally constitutes treason.

We the People reserve the right to revise and extend the list of federal government arrogations, violations, and usurpations as they are brought to our attention for remediation in our State courts and/or through reform legislation.

After almost 150 years of federal abuse and arrogation, We the People have thought ourselves powerless, our creature having amassed a limitless ocean of cash coerced from our honest labor; plunging us into a worse servitude than that which caused our forefathers to rebel against British tyranny, and new laws spawning socialist schemes repugnant to American values.

We have thought ourselves having no voice in matters of life, liberty, property, or trillion-dollar rackings of the economy. As the creators of our federal government designed to serve us and our States, we have long acted as its pawns, bereft of hope.

But no more.

We the People declare our resolve to enforce the Law of the Land under the 9th Amendment, in which we retained all powers not specifically enumerated to federal government.

As the apex sovereigns in American government, we citizens intend to perennially prosecute our members of Congress who violate the Constitution. We will tighten the chains of the Constitution's *specifically* enumerated powers; as is our right and power to do, we will allow *no implication* beyond said powers.

We realize that our present level of public awareness and discourse is abysmal, yet we do not despise the day of small beginnings. The wheels of State justice may grind slowly in our newly-discovered 9th and 10th Amendment enforcement mechanism, but this shall not dim our determination.

We the People will call our corrupt member of Congress home from building his personal estate; from doing the bidding of powerful individuals behind the scenes, and we will bring civil or criminal actions for violations of our State statutes that happen to be committed while the perpetrator is a member Congress. Violations of the politician's State statutes are exclusive original and appellate jurisdiction of the Courts of the State in which the parties reside.

Our plaintiff groups will all be citizens of a common State with the defendant. No State being a party to these actions, nothing in the Constitution can be construed to allow federal courts to steal jurisdiction and free the perpetrator.

Any attempt by a defendant or by federal courts to make either of the following assertions will constitute *fraud and racketeering* to evade enforcement of the 9th and 10th Amendments:

(a) A claim that Taxpayer funds diverted to U.S. Treasury accounts in Washington, D.C., makes a politician's actions an *interstate* issue, federal jurisdiction; or

(b) A claim that any participation or acquiescence in the century-old system of graft, fraud, and racketeering by Congress by our own member of that body and committed against us, the constituents of that member, is a *constitutional* issue, thus within original or appellate jurisdiction of the U.S. Supreme Court.

AmericaAgain! has not made rekindling Militias of the Several States a major priority because we believe that peaceful action under rule of law is more effective. Yet, because millions of citizens today share the founders' concerns about government efforts to disarm citizens, we will no longer shirk our duty. Believing in peace through strength against enemies foreign or domestic, we believe it is incumbent on all good citizens to become prepared and armed in their own homes so that such arms might never be necessary.

To reiterate, the God-given right and pre-constitutional duty of We the People to be properly armed in our own homes and on our own persons for defense, does not require vigilante action. We are opposed to armed collective action (public drills, muster, or practice) until our State Legislatures enact Militia legislation as is assumed in the Second Amendment.

We expect to be fortified by grand juries, prosecutors, and courts of our Sovereign States, and by our constables, sheriffs, state troopers, rangers, and state guard troops who must not be intimidated from their duty to *'preserve, protect, and defend the Constitution'* but who must now enforce it by giving teeth to the long-abdicated 9th and 10th Amendments.

We the People of America will not be governed by what other nations may do. Even among us 50 sovereign States, we are distinct governments and cultures. In league with all people of the world who want to live in peace without tyranny, we seek to be good stewards of the natural resources that God has entrusted to us. But we do not subscribe to politically-correct, increasingly disproven claims of scientists whose continued funding depends on whipping citizens into perpetual frenzy.

We trust God's providence for our future; we do not trust politicians, bureaucrats, and the powerful cabal who have owned them since Lincoln's time.

This tactical project of We the People of these sovereign States shall not be co-opted, overseen, joined, or infested by politicians, lobbyists, or operatives from any level of government or by any political party, foreign or domestic.

America was founded as a Christian – not Jewish, Muslim, or atheist – commonwealth. An honest survey of America's original documents of government, law, economics, or social life prove that America is founded on Christianity and no other belief system. Not all beliefs produce equally efficacious or humane law, ethics, or economics. Ideas have consequences.

We the People seek to keep our government free from theocracy. History illustrates that self-styled Christians have oppressed and killed in the name of religion, but because Mohammed's teachings have the starkest record of bloody oppression when it controls, we will outlaw Islam's strategic plan to infest our States as it has done in other societies.

We will organize and operate locally as free citizens in the privacy of our homes, businesses, churches, parks, and any venue that suits us as owners and residents of such places, without government oversight, infiltration, or coercion that is common in tyrannical regimes yet we will not operate in any unlawful, seditious, riotous, rebellious, or terroristic manner.

Should our member of Congress refuse to stop violating the law; should (s)he prevaricate, obfuscate, or bloviate as politicians often do; should (s)he return to D.C. to conspire anew with like-minded scoundrels and moneyed oligarchs who purchased his/her first allegiance – we will pursue his/her criminal conviction in our State Courts.

If (s)he refuses to obey the Supreme Law of the Land, we will seek the longest possible State Penitentiary term for him/her.

As actual and punitive damages for multi-trillion-dollar fraud and conspiracy, we will have our State Court seize any and all of his/her assets held under any structure whatsoever, in any jurisdiction in the world whatsoever, inuring to the benefit of the member of Congress or his/her family or descendants.

To any State grand jury, prosecutor, judge, constable, sheriff or other State official who refuses (whether by complicity, timidity, coercion, or subornation) to oversee justice as their oath demands – We The People shall seek your impeachment and seat your replacement to restore rule of law.

No defendant who serves in Congress can plead ignorance of the abovegoing facts of history and the Constitution, nor ignorance of federal laws over which (s)he is responsible or for which (s)he voted, yet has not read. Ignorance of the law is not a defense for members of Congress, who are charged with enacting laws, and sworn to support the Constitution.

We the People offer our member of Congress immunity from indictment if and only if (s)he, in writing with notarized witnesses from among our AmericaAgain! membership, agrees to: withdraw support for or acquiescence in the aforesaid violations of the Constitution; sponsor or co-sponsor the legislation outlined above, drafted by citizens and submitted for his/her consideration; propose or support no amendment thereto except as approved by the local or State AmericaAgain! chapter should such exist, after said citizen bod(ies) have had sufficient time to review said amendment.

This citizens' effort called AmericaAgain! has been conceived by regular citizens of the sovereign States of America. We believe that in America, by God's grace, a diligent minority of 'mere' citizens can restore liberty, property, rule of law, and the sovereignty of our households and free States guaranteed in the 9th and 10th Amendments.

Each member of Congress has left a public record in history. By their response to citizens now enforcing the Constitution that they have so long violated, they now demonstrate their repentant fidelity, or their ignominious corruption.

We give thanks to God and ask His blessing on this formerly godly republic, that we may be AmericaAgain!

We The People of these fifty united States
Original draft offered nationally on
Thanksgiving Day
November 26, 2009

Appendix D:

A Tax Honesty Primer

California transplant Joseph Stack flew his private airplane into the side of the IRS headquarters building in Austin, Texas this morning, after leaving a suicide note to the IRS on an internet forum.

The saddest aspect of this tragedy is not only Mr. Stack's needless death (had he been aware of Tax Honesty, he'd still be alive); the saddest part is not even the fact that today across America, countless thousands of lives are being destroyed, marriages shattered, homes taken, careers ended, and businesses shut down by a 97-year-old terror organization.

The most tragic part of the largest financial crime in American history is that citizens don't realize that <u>Congress</u> perpetrates this terrorist scam. The IRS is just the black-hooded bag-man, whose purpose is to frighten its employers to death. Literally.

Introduction

I've read the Tax Code and cases for 13 years, thrice as long as I studied engineering at university. As a law-abiding Nontaxpayer for 11 years now, I don't fear my employees at the IRS. As one of the estimated *67 million* non-filers in America, I don't worry about today's news cycles or political fights because I no longer have a dog in that fight. I don't allow Nancy Pelosi, Barney Frank, Barry Hussein Obama, Harry Reid, or other corrupt scum to skim my checks for their illicit uses.

This is neither legal nor tax advice. This primer is for Americans like me, who've had our fill of the corrupt, brazen Washington D.C. junta that does anything it wants no matter how illegal, while terrorizing Taxpayers to keep pulling the load like stupid oxen. You're not an ox; you have a brain, and it's not illegal to use it. Americans have God-given freedom of speech, guaranteed by the Constitution. Corrupt government and collusive 'tax professionals' can't stop us from speaking and thinking; *this isn't China.*

This primer does *not* incite law-breaking, violence, or even tar-and-feathers for thieves in Congress or their bag-men at IRS. When a government becomes as massive and corrupt as Washington D.C., the last thing we need is lawless citizens trying to counterpunch. We need rule of law for *everyone.*

The Internet is the great leveler against corrupt, powerful people who have enslaved working citizens for many generations. It doesn't take many courageous, self-governing citizens to turn the tide of history. Even if most people are afraid of their employees, we can enjoy more liberty than our great-grandparents knew.

Compare the federal budget's allocations with the 17 enumerated powers we granted our federal creature in Article I Section 8 of the Constitution. About 75% of current federal expenditures are for items not enumerated among its lawful powers, enabling Washington D.C. to regulate every area of life.

For 150 years, Congress has become increasingly like every other government on earth, a shakedown racket. Still, this corruption by Taxspenders is *financially enabled by Taxpayers*. Congress didn't increase the size and powers of federal Leviathan by 1000% in just two generations by magic. To paraphrase an irreverent line from Bill Clinton's staff: *it's the money, stupid.*

Think about a typical spoiled brat; the child may be a piece of work, but we know that *the parents are to blame*. The massive, out-of-control government that millions of citizens love to complain about only exists because *Taxpayers keep sending in trillions every year*. Legal or illegal expenditure? It doesn't matter; bureaucrats and functionaries either spend it this year or get less next year. This is the way with government, including the bloated, bureaucratic military machine that President Eisenhower warned us of in 1961.

A federal government limited to the enumerated (lawful) powers we gave it in the Constitution should require $400-$750 billion annually, depending on the extent of military expenditure one assumes for national defense and global intelligence. We should never be talking about a $1 trillion federal budget, much less this tsunami that is approaching *$4 trillion* annually!

Earth's Largest Crime Cartel

> *Silence can only be equated with fraud where there is a legal or moral duty to speak, or where an inquiry left unanswered would be intentionally misleading... We cannot condone this shocking behavior by the IRS. Our revenue system is based on the good faith of the taxpayer and the taxpayers should be able to expect the same from the government in its enforcement and collection activities.* **U.S. v. Tweel, 550 F.2d 297, 299. See also U.S. v. Prudden, 424 F.2d 1021, 1032; Carmine v. Bowen, 64 A. 932.**

Forget the War on Drugs...Washington, D.C. runs earth's largest crime cartel. In cash equivalent and corrupting power, the present federal revenues take equals over 10,000 major drug cartels operating inside the D.C. beltway.

Law-abiding Nontaxpayers no longer support that criminal enterprise. After I proved to myself that the Tax Code is perfectly constitutional, I had no problem with the Code. I obey it, and I make IRS obey it as well.

This primer will explain what I have researched, and found, and what I believe about taxation. You'll see why I came to the conclusions I came to; why the IRS hasn't touched one dollar in my accounts or one hair on my head in 11 years although I've been very vocal with them by certified mail all those years.

The Best Book Exposing Congress' Tax Scam

Throughout this primer, I'll mention Phil Hart, a fellow professional engineer and former Idaho State representative. His book, *Constitutional Income: Do You Have Any?* is in its 3rd printing, an invaluable resource to help you learn how Congress hatched its IRS scam during the period 1909-13.

Hart did a great deal of investigative journalism in the matter of Congressional fraud and theft. This should have been done long ago by the American press, were it not so terrorized by Congress' Gestapo. Mr. Hart dug out relevant rulings, news articles, and congressional memos from those critical four years when Congress gave birth to a two-headed beast: its Federal Reserve counterfeiting concession, and its IRS scam to mop up the excess liquidity created by that geyser of worthless 'money', to avoid hyperinflation.

Hart's book can save you years of research, and avoid silly 'tax protestor' theories and terror threats from tax industry shills. If you read this primer, plus Phil Hart's book with highlighter in hand, and the two analytical websites I will mention below, you'll know more about Congress' IRS scam than most of America's CPAs and tax preparers.

IRS Practices Evasion Every Day

I've owned marked-up copies of the Tax Code, and have enjoyed studying tax law and history for over a decade. As I said earlier, I haven't filed IRS forms or paid income taxes in eleven years, after getting nothing but Tax Honesty evasion from the following among our employees at IRS: Michael Thomas and Nancy Sessions (IRS Austin); Beverly Coogan and Aaron Hamor (IRS San Antonio); R.A. Mitchell, C. Sherwood, Grace Metro, and Debra K. Hurst (IRS Dallas); Dennis Parizek and Deborah Egan (IRS Ogden); Susan Meredith (IRS Fresno); Teresa Webb (IRS Memphis); Stephanie Borop and Queen Vaughn (IRS Nashville).

I wrote to them via certified mail, asking: *Where is the section of law making me legally liable for keeping records, filing returns, and paying your demands? Many things are called out as taxable activities in the Code, but most aren't...including my line of work. So can you show me where the law creates a liability for my gainful activity, as it does for all those others?*

In all the years I've been a law-abiding Nontaxpayer, all the IRS operatives listed above have engaged in willful tax honesty evasion, sending one of these non-responses: our dog ate my homework *("we haven't finished our research, we'll get back to you")* or hot potato *("we forwarded your request to the office shown below")*. In law, this is known as fraud and conspiracy.

After 11 years of being very vocal with them on this point, IRS has not touched me, my money, or my property. They have, however, committed several indictable acts of fraud according to the Texas Penal Code. But I'll cover that later; let's go one step at a time.

Some People ARE Made Liable in the Code

Notice I'm not suggesting that there's no law making *anyone* liable for income tax. Shortly, I'll show you many categories of domicile or activity that *is* called out in the Tax Code as having a duty. Tax

Honesty does not say *"there's no law!"* as some IRS defenders caricature it. I simply say that the Tax Code is specific, I obey it, and I make my federal employees obey it also.

How Did Income Taxes Spring Up in One Generation?

Read Phil Hart's book to find out; also, the Donald Duck article on the Tax Honesty Primer blog http://taxhonestyprimer.blogspot.com/2010/02/many-greedy-hands.html

Amity Schlaes concluded the same in her book *The Greedy Hand.* It seemed odd to me: tax industry apologists and gurus claim that the 16th Amendment made everyone liable, but the history of tax revenues don't support the assertion. The 16th Amendment was passed in 1913, yet it took *a generation* for most Americans to be snookered into believing it was their duty to fund a RICO scam.

Mr. Hart's book will make you furious at Congress – and at tax accountants and attorneys. If you become an AmericaAgain! member, you'll become prepared to start *doing something* about all the criminal activity in Congress.

"The sky is blue" is not a *position*

You won't find theories or my 'beliefs' in this Primer; only rulings of the U.S. Supreme Court, citations from the Internal Revenue Code, Code of Federal Regulations, Internal Revenue Manual, Black's Law Dictionary, and Sutherland's Rules of Statutory Construction; names of former IRS agents, attorneys, auditors; quotes from an IRS Commissioner; and testimony from the Historian of the IRS appearing before a congressional committee.

A few housekeeping points

Before we go into the red-pill adventure in the Tax Code, cases, and supporting evidence and rulings I'll chase off cockroaches with a few points of housekeeping:

<u>Point #1</u> Tax Honesty is the opposite of 'tax protesting'; it is responsible citizenship. It's neither anti-government nor anti-tax; rather, Tax Honesty is anti-corruption and anti-terrorist.

<u>Point #2</u> As a corollary to Point #1, we all agree that lawful taxation is necessary to fund the lawful functions of government.

<u>Point #3</u> Tax-theory gurus will continue to be convicted for selling loopy theories, but Tax Honesty doesn't support tax-protest theories, theories about the 16th Amendment, theories like "wages aren't income", or continuing to file as a taxpayer but demanding refunds or filling in all zeroes. Nontaxpayers must not take "positions" or seek to do away with the IRS or the Tax Code. I support the Federal Tax Code exactly as it is written.

<u>Point #4</u> For detailed data-mining of the Tax Code and federal regulations, see the website *www.whatistaxed.com* and for an exhaustive formal logic and legal analysis of the scam, see the website *www. synapticsparks.info/*.

<u>Point #5</u> If you work in the tax industry (government or private-sector) and want to leave the Axis of Evil, I'm happy to answer your e-mails. But don't e-mail to debate me; you're defending a scam and I took the red pill. *Go pound sand.* Your threat *"I'll visit you in prison!"* is ludicrous.

First, out of 67 million non-filers, fewer than 250 are even *recommended* for indictment by IRS annually; they're people who: 1) demand refunds, 2) file and sign things but then refuse to pay, or 3) follow wacky theories. Second, IRS recommends *eight times as many filers* for indictment each year as non-filers. So with 67 million non-filers to 115 million filers, that means you'll visit *four* of your filer friends in prison before you visit *one* non-filer like me there.

Learn how your profession has slumped towards Gomorrah in Mike Brewster's book *Unaccountable: How the Accounting Profession Forfeited a Public Trust.* If you intend to continue holding clients down while IRS does bad things to them, don't delude yourself that you're an honest professional performing a needed service.

The annual Tax Terror Season

If you're still a Taxpayer, you're **terrorized** by your employees at IRS because they drag out a few high-profile 'tax cheat' trophies every Tax Terror Season, from January 1 until April 15.

It's the same idea your CPA or tax preparer uses when they repeat the "death and taxes" line: the tax industry plays good cop to IRS's bad cop. Your Taxpayer heart pounds, you borrow the money for the next IRS payment, your CPA makes his Lexus payment, and you trudge ahead in the *fair share* line.

Dinosaur government and tax professionals in the tar pit

According to a former IRS Fraud Examiner (later Tax Honesty spokeswoman), there were 67 million non-filers as of 2005 compared with 'only' 30 million non-filers by Commissioner Rosotti's 1998 estimate. That's an astounding growth rate. With an estimated 110 million filers, this means that at least one in three Americans is no longer underwriting the corrupt Congress' bailout and check-skimming machine.

As James Davidson and Lord William Rees-Mogg predicted ten years ago in their book *The Sovereign Individual* – the internet is making bureaucratic, redistributionist governments unsustainable; in America as in Europe, the dinosaurs are in the tar-pit.

Today's financial news signifies the struggle for survival between Taxpayers and Taxspenders; this battle is reaching critical mass in The Age of Obama. In the Bush II era, we saw textbook *fascism:* massive expansion of the police state and military, restrictions on liberty of travel, eavesdropping on our calls and emails, and more. Now in Obamanation, we see textbook *socialism:* the destruction of private property, nationalization of industries, and crippling new regulation and taxation to make slaves pay for their own chains!

This is a critical phase in modern history: the D.C. al Qaeda will attempt to stay alive and grow like cancer into every area of life where it doesn't already control. Even as millions of Americans become Nontaxpayers, millions of Taxpayers are going broke, live under IRS duress or 'payment plans'; they curse life in America and wonder where on earth they can move to, to just be left alone! This is un-American, and just *wrong.*

It's not only injustice; it's 'professionals' abetting corruption. These industry operatives help the U.S. Congress obscure the real issues; they appeal to collusive federal judges' rulings about 'frivolous tax protestors'.

But something is happening in America and around the world. *Pushback.* Here in America, the Tea Party movement and the heated battle about government's attempted socialist takeover of healthcare, are just facets of a world trend against Leviathan. The Internet is liberating citizens to dig up corruption, and fight it.

The *takers* seek a good life at taxpayer expense; parasites found in every housing project, welfare line, illegal alien safehouse, military retirement plan, legal and accounting office, congressman's and senator's lair, and every meeting of ACORN or MoveOn.org. Taxpayers are now at the breaking point, joining Tax Honesty... America's *real* War on Terror.

No law makes the *average* American liable for income tax

Does that statement sound unbelievable? It's been asserted and proven to juries across America over two decades:

Thomas Reeves of Paducah, KY made the same assertion in 1988; the jury *acquitted* him. Franklin Sanders and (16) co-defendants in the Memphis area made this assertion in 1991; the jury *acquitted* them. Gabriel Scott of Fairbanks, AK made this assertion in 1992; the jury *acquitted* him. Lloyd Long of Chattanooga, TN made this assertion in 1993; the jury *acquitted* him. Frederick and Christopher Allnut of Baltimore, MD made this assertion in 1996; the jury *acquitted* them. Gaylon Harrell of Logan County, IL made this assertion in 2000; the jury *acquitted* him. Donald Fecay of Detroit, MI made this assertion in 2001; the jury *acquitted* him. Vernice Kuglin of Memphis, TN made this assertion in 2003; the jury *acquitted* her. Dr. Lois Somerville of Lake Mary, FL made this assertion in 2003; U.S. District Judge Patricia C. Fawsett *acquitted* her. Former Treasury Department CID agent Joe Banister made this assertion in 2005; the jury *acquitted* him. Attorney Thomas Cryer of Shreveport, LA made this assertion in 2007; the jury *acquitted* him.

I don't listen to freeloaders who put a guilt trip on those who don't file, suggesting that "Nontaxpayers don't pay their 'fair share' for roads, schools, and trash pickup." I learned what all those jurors learned: *those things are not funded by federal tax revenues.*

Do you believe in the Tax Fairy?

The law and the IRS can be left exactly as they are, with just one simple change: IRS employees must obey the law and not commit fraud or extortion. Don't fall for the politicians' pitch about a coming 'solution' that they call *Fair Tax*. In truth, a national sales tax would carry America from the frying pan into the fire.

America's Parasite Sector: IRS is the tip of the iceberg

Ask anyone who invested with Ponzi-schemer Bernard Madoff: the very nature of successful fraud is that *it does actually defraud.* The mark actually believes the fraudster, sometimes for many years. So this will be weirder than hearing that your spouse of 25 years has been cheating on you since your wedding night...stranger than finding out that your best friend is an axe-murderer. *Cognitive dissonance* is what happens when everything you ever knew about something is turned upside down.

You may get a bit light-headed and confused; that's normal. When you start considering doing something about it, if you're not very courageous you may get anxiety attacks and lose sleep. That's normal too.

Upton Sinclair said *"It is difficult to get a man to understand something when his salary depends upon his not understanding it."* Your CPA may refuse to discuss Tax Honesty, threatening "I'll see you in prison!". He doesn't want his professional career exposed as corrupt; what do you *expect* him to say? Defenders of *"pay your taxes"* are legion. Congress' IRS scam is almost impossible to expose because it feeds a *massive* parasite population that you've likely never considered.

Most of us produce something of use to others, or we fix things, or grow things, or sell useful stuff. But there are literally tens of millions of parasite-sector Americans:

- corrupt politicians including federal judges
- their bloated staffs and other bureaucrats
- thousands of govt contractors employing tens of millions
- IRS employees
- large accounting firms and individual accountants
- tax law firms and their employees
- tax software companies
- tax training (seminar & publishing) companies
- tax preparation services
- university endowments in tax law & accounting
- tax-deferred investment groups
- tax-shelter mutual funds
- the tax shelter real estate sector
- equipment, vehicle, and aircraft leasing companies
- manufacturers and vendors of all depreciable equipment

- IRS 'workout' services that advertise "we're former IRS agents" and the two *really big Kahunas:*
- America's mortgage industry
- America's non-profit industry, religious and secular

Had you ever seen the connection to all those industries? Now you know why you hear "pay your taxes" and "render unto Caesar" from counselors who've enjoyed great public trust and respect. If they run from Tax Honesty, they don't deserve that trust and respect; they've chosen *parasitic* life.

In an interview in the May 25, 1956 issue of *U.S. News & World Report,* IRS Commissioner T. Coleman Andrews said, *"There is a veritable army of people, organizations and businesses with a powerful vested interest in keeping the noses of the rest of us to the grindstone...let no one underestimate the power of the* [tax industry]. *"*

Loopy Tax Protestor Gurus vs. Evil Tax Industry Gurus

I repeat, *this is not legal or tax advice.* Learn as you read, and don't let this be all you read. Take everything with a grain of salt; test statements against one another and against the law as written.

With respect to the income tax, law means *the actual words* of the Tax Code; nothing else is law. Not an IRS letter or demand, and not an IRS pamphlet or flyer about "your rights as a Taxpayer". Those are P.R. eyewash from an administrative branch agency, the stimulus gang's bag men. IRS publications have no legal weight. IRS employees must obey the law, as you and I must. Remember that, the next time your employees attempt to terrorize you.

I also don't trust 'tax protestor' theories and those who peddle them. As I did my research over the years, I found a great deal of hokum in the early Tax Honesty movement, some of which was probably accurately termed *tax protesting.* I found a gazillion theories: twisting a quote or ruling out of context; making up bizarre theories about capitalization; about admiralty law; about the UCC; about wages not being income; about U.S. citizenship being of the devil; about the Tax Code being unconstitutional; about Section 861 being a secret silver bullet; about filing all zeroes...

I stick to the law as written; rulings that make sense in context. I follow the money trail to see how Leviathan got here. As an engineer, I like things to make sense... *Occam's Razor* and all that.

When you reach the citations of U.S. Supreme Court rulings below, and you're trying to decide who has more clout in the system, keep the following section of the Internal Revenue Manual in mind:

Internal Revenue Manual
4.10.7.2.9.8
Importance of Court Decisions

A case decided by the U.S. Supreme Court becomes the law of the land and takes precedence over decisions of lower courts. The Internal Revenue Service must follow Supreme Court decisions. For examiners, Supreme Court decisions have the same weight as the Code.

The U.S. Supreme Court trumps anybody at the IRS. Try to keep that in mind as you read this.

AAAaaaauuuuugh!! I can't find my socks!!!

Whether you're a filer or non-filer, you should own a current copy of the Tax Code. Don't waste hundreds of hours being dragged by the nose through Congress's maze of smoke and mirrors; instead:

a) buy a copy of the latest IRC (I use Thomson Reuters single-volume edition)
http://ria.thomsonreuters.com/estore/detail.aspx?ID=IR7P&SITE=/taxresearch/federal

b) buy a highlighter and a set of color-coded plastic index tabs

c) go to a website called *The Tax Code For All* to see the mere (124) lines in the Code that specifically indicate activities imposing a legal duty to keep records, file, and pay. *www.taxcodeforall.blogspot.com*

Highlight and tab those sections. Don't believe the tax industry line about how "huge and confusing" the Tax Code is. They just want you to stay terrorized and confused.

Here's a fitting analogy: when Smith wants to buy some new socks from Sears, does he fall on the floor in a tearful heap wailing *"AAAaaaauuuugh!! That confounded 10,000-page catalog!! No American can understand it!! Even the people who wrote it can't give me a straight answer!!! It's HUGE!! Waaaaaaaaaahh!!"* ?

Of course not. That would be very silly. Smith just opens the catalog to the page for men's socks, orders what he needs, and treats the gazillions of other things in the huge catalog as if they don't exist. It's the same with laws, including the Tax Code. If a law doesn't apply to who you are or what you do, then you can treat that law as though it doesn't exist.

As you'll witness the U.S. Supreme Court ruling repeatedly below, and the Internal Revenue Manual demanding of every IRS employee below – laws of taxation must be clear, and the person from whom a tax is sought must be shown in *specific language* to be taxable. Everyone else can just leave the big, fat book aside; it doesn't apply to them.

My CPAs over the years, if they had been competent and honest, should have known that it never had applied to me. But most in 'the system' won't tell you that because they're like nerds with pocket protectors standing in every aisle at Sears. Huge catalog in hand, their career is showing you what page to look on so you can buy your socks. If you figure out the game, they're out of work. Don't expect them to support Tax Honesty. We're all human. Even pirates need to eat.

As with every law, Tax Code applies to certain subjects only

As you'll see presently, well-settled law including U.S. Supreme Court rulings over a century hold that *when a tax law lists some things as taxable, then things NOT listed are NOT taxable.*

As I read the citations below, according to the U.S. Supreme Court, the law must specifically point out what activities are taxable.

With my Tax Code marked up to show specifically listed taxable activities, I confirmed what the law requires of a 'taxpayer'; who the law makes a 'taxpayer' as opposed to the claims of the CPA, H&R Block guy, IRS employee, or tax dishonesty guru Dan Evans.

A common response from those in the system when Tax Honesty arises is, 'Render unto Caesar!'. But obviously we're not ancient Rome; we're not ruled by Caesars. We're ruled by our federal and State Constitutions and all laws made pursuant to them.

The Internal Revenue Code (26 USC) is the codification of the statutes that establish a legal duty for certain people to keep records, file forms, and pay income tax...but only those people whose activities or situations meet the taxing provisions in the Code, according to the U.S. Supreme Court, and Black's Law Dictionary, and Sutherland's Rules of Statutory Construction.

Thus, as I see it, any person who meets those Tax Code provisions specifically called out in law, but refuses to pay the taxes stipulated is properly called a tax evader. Anyone not made liable in the specific language of the Tax Code is free to be a Nontaxpayer, legally free to ignore that law as (s)he ignores all other law codes that don't apply to him or her.

IRS Whistleblowers

The *Code of Ethics for Government Service* requires any government employee or official who obtains evidence of a government violation of law to report it, not to cover it up or participate as a conspirator, as IRS employees do every day. A government official or employee who violates laws is not to be obeyed but reported for those violations and indicted where applicable.

The IRS has had a few honest and courageous employees over the years. In her sworn testimony before the Senate Finance Committee in 1997, Shelley L. Davis, the only official IRS Historian in the history of that agency, said the IRS is systemically lawless and corrupt. Former IRS employees have learned the truth about Congress' IRS scam, left the agency and are now spokesmen for Tax Honesty including Treasury and CID agent Joe Banister, IRS agents Clifton Beale and John Turner, IRS fraud examiner Sherry Jackson, IRS attorney Paul Chappell, and IRS auditor Matthew McErlean.

In his 1956 interview, IRS Commissioner Andrews said,

> *I don't like the income tax...every time we talk about these taxes we get the idea of 'from each according to his capacity and to each according to his needs.' That's socialism! It's written into the Communist Manifesto... Maybe we ought to see that everybody who gets a tax return receives... a Communist Manifesto with it, so he can see what's happening to him.*

The heart of the trap: "Everybody has to pay their taxes!"

I'm not a tax lawyer, CPA, tax accountant, nor do I offer legal or tax advice. I'm a follower of Christ first, a Texan second and an American third. We have the God-given right to speak about our rights and duties for self-government; the government and tax industry practitioners and terrorists can't restrict that right.

Perhaps your HR manager, CPA, or tax preparer has shown you the Tax Code section, *"...every individual having for the taxable year..."* and suggests that this means every person that makes money, saying everybody has to pay 'their taxes'. Well, yes and no; it's an ambiguous statement.

I do have to pay 'my taxes' if that means every sales tax, excise tax, property tax, import duty, etc... that I owe by law. But I don't have to pay 'my taxes' as defined by the fraudulent, mercenary tax industry, even if not found in law. The tax industry and online gurus who inveigh against Tax Honesty love to peddle the lie that the Tax Code reads like the <u>Revenue Act of 1894</u>:

> *"There shall be assessed, levied, collected, and paid annually upon the gains, profits, and income received in the preceding calendar year by every citizen of the United States . . . from any profession, trade, employment, or vocation carried on in the United States or elsewhere, or from any other source what-soever, a tax."*

Can't be any more all-encompassing than that, right? If everybody just owed a tax, the Tax Code would be about half a page long, right? Everybody has to pay, period. But that's an extortionist's lie.

As Phil Hart explains in his book, the income tax scheme was devised by a very sneaky Congress after the Supreme Court ruled that the language above was unconstitutional. To hide the truth (that very few occupations trigger a Tax Code liability section), the crooks in Congress made the Code increasingly large and complex.

Still, it appears to me that beneath those tens of thousands of pages of gobbledygook the Code is as it always was: very limited in its scope, just as the framers meant internal taxation to be.

As the US Supreme Court has *repeatedly* ruled, it only applies to activities *specifically called out* in the law; to persons having taxable income. Persons made liable for an income tax in the Code; persons defined in Section 7701(a)14 as Taxpayers.

Are income taxes voluntary? An entrapment scheme?

How could so many people be so blind to fraud and theft of this magnitude? Well, in the first place, I began to realize (as I showed you) how many industries and careers are in cahoots pushing the propaganda. Parasites need to eat, just as productive people do. So it makes sense that a lot of people insist that everyone paying income taxes is a legal duty.

But some people maintain that income taxes are voluntary, basing their theory on snippets of rulings like that in the 1960 Flora case:

> *Our system of taxation is based upon voluntary assessment and payment, not upon distraint.* **Flora v. United States, 362 U.S. 176 (1960)**

What does that ruling mean? I think those who claim that all income tax is just voluntary are reading too much into *Flora*. Obviously, for anyone whose activities are specifically listed in the Tax Code, paying income taxes is not voluntary!

I was flabbergasted when I discovered the practical meaning of the court's words in Flora. For 20 years I really had been volunteering, in a way. Defrauded and terrorized by Congress and the tax industry, I never engaged in any activity specifically called out in the Tax Code. Some activities are listed in the Code as having a legal duty to keep records, file, and pay, but my gainful activities aren't listed anywhere. For two decades, I was just self-assessing and signing promissory documents under penalty of perjury without ever seeing a copy of the Code, much less reading it. I was just doing what everybody else did.

The court did not say in *Flora* that even if by law I don't owe a tax, that once I self-assess, sign under penalty of perjury, and mail the tax return, that I owe what I promise anyway! That would be fraud, extortion, and entrapment.

Okay...so what is going on with all you filers? Is it government fraud and entrapment for 115 million people to file things without looking into the Tax Code even the least bit? Is it government fraud and entrapment for a Taxpayer to let the state and federal Leviathan skim 40% of his livelihood, without seeing if he ever owed it by law? It's technically extortion and racketeering, but still: you the Taxpayer have failed to perform due diligence as a free, self-governing citizen under American law.

Call it ignorance, or apathy, or state-sponsored terror. There are still 67 million of us that aren't drinking the Kool-Aid, and don't have CPAs telling us what we 'must do by law' so they can keep their cushy careers. No population can live in fear of its public servants yet honestly call itself free.

I helped destroy our constitutional republic as an ignorant filer, funding criminals for 20 years. I now feel it my duty to host this free Tax Honesty Primer to atone for decades of abdication. I study to learn how this republic of sovereign States and sovereign People was transformed into a socialist empire of mobsters at the federal, state, county, city, and school board levels – now joined by a huge parasitic private sector as well.

So what made me a Taxpayer all those years?

First I had to ask myself: was I a Taxpayer? That may seem like a silly question, but it's the first critical lynch-pin upon which Congress had been hanging my checkbook for 20 years.

The Internal Revenue Code defines taxpayer as *"any person subject to any internal revenue tax"* at 26 USC 7701(a)14, and as *"any person subject to a tax under the applicable revenue law"* at 26 USC 1313(b). But I could never find a section making me subject to the tax.

After over a dozen demands, all of those IRS employees listed by name above refused to supply me with any part of the Code showing a section of law establishing a legal duty in the Code for me or almost anybody else, for that matter.

The 'Taxable Income' position

Some books and websites teach the 'taxable income' line of inquiry, and in fact that line of reasoning was what led former IRS CID agent Joe Banister to leave the IRS.

But I didn't want to play Congress' semantic games: taxable income is defined in terms of 'adjusted gross income' in Section 63... 'adjusted gross income' is defined in terms of a 'taxpayer' in Section 62a...and Section 6012(a) reads, *"Returns with respect to income taxes under Subtitle A shall by made by . . . every individual having for the taxable year gross income,"* etc. Then, 'individual' is defined in the regulations...and to have a 'taxable year' one must be not only an 'individual', but a 'taxpayer' according to Section 441(b)(1).

The whole thing is a spaghetti-bowl maze. Corrupt members of Congress trying to keep trillions coming in every year, must render the law more confusing to the 'target' until (s)he just gives up, self-assesses like the neighbors do, and pays up.

I went back to looking for who is a Taxpayer; where does the law impose a legal duty on me where I live, doing what I do? By law they have to do so; why wouldn't IRS employees just show me *that?* Because *it doesn't exist.*

26USC A(1)(A)(I)(1)...the favorite semantic trap

Most HR managers make a very short discussion out of it; they trot out the very first sentence in the body of the Tax Code...Subtitle A, Chapter 1, Subchapter A, Part I, Section 1: *There is hereby imposed on the taxable income of every married individual... .*

Well, that was easy; everybody owes 'their' taxes, see? Not quite; remember, the Supreme Court ruled that a universal tax is unconstitutional. They made the corrupt Congress return what it had sucked in under unconstitutional 'everybody owes' language.

The snakes had to find a different path to your wallet; they did so with help from their partners in accounting, law, and tax preparation; they added miles of convoluted word games so that no sane person would take on the Tax Code on his own.

For instance, this word *individual* is an interesting example of fraudulent drafting. Congress pulled this semantic trick because definitions in laws can have a very different meaning from what the same word means in regular conversation. So take another step down the rabbit hole to see how Congress appears to be taxing everyone, while not actually doing that. If they can use a trick word in just the right place, they won't get their hand slapped again by the Supreme Court.

The Tax Code right up front says that every _individual_ has a tax imposed. How does Congress define the word _individual_ in the Tax Code? Hmmmm... It _doesn't_. But the Federal Regulations do define _individual:_

26 CFR 1.1441-1
Requirement for deduction and withholding of tax on payments to foreign persons.

(c) Definitions
(3) Individual.
(i) _Alien_ individual. The term alien individual means an individual who is not a citizen...
(ii) Nonresident _alien_ individual. The term nonresident alien individual means a person described in section 7701(b)(1)(B), an alien individual who is...

****

Notice, just _aliens_. The regulation only stipulates _foreign_ persons. If you suggest _"don't look there, you ninny; that says 'foreign persons' in the heading"_ I challenge you to see where else the law or regulations define 'individual'; you won't find it anywhere else. [I used search engines on the Tax Code and Federal Regulations. It was easy online to do a Boolean word search for _individual_ in the text of the Tax Code. I used the government's own websites, and I also used _www. whatistaxed.com_ to do the data-mining exercise.]

Criminals in Congress devised a way to write law so that wasn't unconstitutional yet could still catch almost every fish, like dynamite. I didn't need to pursue the semantic games to prove to myself beyond reasonable doubt that I was never a Taxpayer except as I was defrauded into filing. Those bent multi-millionaires in Congress are *shrewd*. What a simple scam, all those years: I self-assessed and signed, becoming what I claimed to be – a Taxpayer – under penalty of perjury! *Congress is simply criminal.*

Yes, they deviously wrote this law, but the law didn't enslave me; my own ignorance and apathy – or terror – enslaved me all those years. I self-assessed and signed returns for all those years without ever having even seen a copy of the Tax Code. Congress' perfect crime has run for 97 years now only because Taxpayers are terrorized and/or ignorant. We have a duty to overcome both!

Who must provide Form W-4 or W-9?

I've asked IRS a dozen times where the Code says that I must, by law, file returns. The law and their operations manual stipulate that they MUST give me an answer, yet in 11 years they've given me nothing but evasion. These are all violations of law and their operating rules in the IRM. They refuse to respond, so I tell them to pound sand every time they bother me.

I've also been asked over the years: which payors are required by law to obtain a W-4, W-9, or a TIN? The only place I have found is Title 26 of the Code of Federal Regulations, stipulating who has a legal duty to furnish a number in response to such a request:

26 CFR 301.6109-1

> *(c) If the person making the return, statement, or other document does not know the taxpayer identifying number of the other person, <u>and such other person is one that is described in paragraph (b)(2)(i), (ii), (iii), or (vi) of this section</u>, such person must request the other person's number. The request should state that the identifying number is required to be furnished under authority of law.*

(b)(2)(i): *A <u>foreign</u> person that has...*
(b)(2)(ii): *A <u>foreign</u> person that has...*

(b)(2)(iii): *A <u>nonresident alien</u> treated as…*
(b)(2)(vi): *A <u>foreign</u> person that…*

Notice, as with the definition of individual, the federal regulation is here only dealing with *foreign persons.*

The Rabbit-Trails Go On Forever

These are just a few semantic traps along the rational trail from Tax Code A(1)A(I)(1) on. Following such trails always left me stuck at 'taxable income' or at 'gross income'…going in circles. Congress and the complicit parasite sector are sneaky; they make it appear that everybody has to pay but remember: when Congress tried universal tax language in 1894, the court slapped their hand.

I knew that *'everybody has to pay'* doesn't meet the Constitution's apportionment and uniformity tests; the Supreme Court says they can't do that. The law *does not say* everybody has to pay income tax.

The semantic traps are built carefully, making work for the tax industry and confusing Taxpayers.

I visited the excellent *www.synapticsparks.info* site, walking the entire length of the 'gross income' bunny-trail, the 'definition of individual' bunny trail, the 'Section 861' bunny trail. *Fascinating.*

Busting the Ponzi Scheme

As I'll show shortly, legal principle and a century of U.S. Supreme Court rulings hold that *if some kinds of work are listed in a tax law, then a citizen is free unless his work is also found <u>specifically</u> listed in the Tax Code, in clear language.* Tax law must be clear; when it isn't clear and the government can't provide law behind its actions or demands…benefit of the doubt goes to the citizen. This is well-settled law.

Dan Evans is a literal Philadelphia lawyer; the self-proclaimed national 'de-bunker' of Tax Honesty. Evans rests his position on the fact that judges have ruled against several Tax Honesty 'gurus' as he calls them. There are three problems with Mr. Evans' claim:

First, regardless how many federal judges might rule in favor of their own paychecks over yours, the law is on the side of citizens and against the IRS scam (read the Supreme Court rulings and other cites below). Second, of the estimated 67 million non-filers, 99.99% of all non-filers are never indicted, much less convicted of anything. Evans citing a couple of high-profile convictions per year cannot negate 67 million non-filers living free!

Third, just because judges in 1830s America said that a Black slave had to be returned to 'his master', or judges in 1930s Russia said that Stalin was in the right when he murdered 20 million people, didn't make those judges right.

It's not illegal to stop being Bernie Madoff's victim

The rulings outlined below are well-settled law. I obey the law, and I take comfort in these well-settled principles of how to interpret tax law when you disagree with administrative agency operatives.

Although it's scary at first, it's also very liberating. Following the money and reading the well-settled law brought me clarity and, after a few years, brought me peace as well. It took years to come to grips with the reality that I was a terror victim, scammed by a large parasite population (public and private) all my working life.

As it was for victims of the Bernie Madoff Ponzi scheme – it always looks obvious *after* you solve the crime.

IRS hauls a few high-profile citizens into court each year to make the terror show work on your mind. They always choose citizens who follow silly theories, who make big money, or who attempt to get juries to see the semantic traps that Congress built into the law. Most juries won't follow the maze; they'll be envious of the wealthy star or starlet who demands a multi-million-dollar tax refund.

The rest of us 67 million Americans who don't file also don't do kooky theories; we just obey the law as written. We don't ask thugs in a dark alley for a refund.

The law has ALWAYS been on your side

In our system of self-government, We the People are the 'authorities' over government; it's every American's duty to know the basics of laws that affect us; basics of our Constitution, so we can keep government honest and help put crooked government actors in prison. As you read through the rulings below, notice that the federal courts have been on our side all along.

I could have been free years earlier, had I known to read tax law and case rulings. Instead, I was terrorized by the tax industry and by pastors and others whose revenues are tied to tax write-offs.

So who exactly does owe income taxes?

> *The individual, unlike the corporation, cannot be taxed for the mere privilege of existing. . . . The individual's rights to live and own property are natural rights for the enjoyment of which an excise cannot be imposed.* **Redfield v. Fisher, 292 P. 813, 135 Or. 180, 294 P.461, 73 A.L.R. 721 (1931)**

To show a duty for an income tax, the government must first show a statute taxing some activity in which the targeted citizen is engaged; some privilege whose use the citizen enjoys:

> *The income tax is, therefore, not a tax on income as such, It is an excise tax with respect to certain activities and privileges which is measured by reference to the income they produce. The income is not the subject of the tax; it is the basis for determining the amount of tax.* **F. Morse Hubbard, pg 2580 House Congressional Record (3/27/43)**

The federal courts agree that the old 'everybody knows' doctrine can't create legal duty; only operation of law or contract can do so:

The taxpayer must be liable for the tax. Tax liability is a condition precedent to the demand. Merely demanding payment, even repeatedly, does not cause liability. **Boathe v. Terry, 713 F.2d 1405, at 1414 (1983)**

No matter how angry and terroristic they got, IRS couldn't create liability for me. I finally realised that these people are my administrative-branch employees, not some judicial body ruling over me. I knew that the IRS can't *write* laws; like you and I and every member of Congress, they must *obey* laws. So I kept going down that rabbit trail; I wanted to see who the Tax Code says has to file returns:

Section 6012.
Persons required to make returns of income.

(1)(A) Every individual having for the taxable year a gross income of the exemption amount or more...

Oh brother; there's that word again. We saw what *individual* means as federal regulations define it...only in terms of *aliens* and since it's defined there and nowhere else, that's the binding legal definition of *individual* for purposes of income taxes.

But I wanted to know...surely some people have to pay income taxes; who are those people? 'Taxpayer' is defined in 7701(a)14 as one *who is subject to any internal revenue law,* so the easiest thing is to just find a section or sections of the Tax Code making some people subject to it. The Supreme Court ruled that according to the Constitution, *everybody* can't be subject to it.

So I'll repeat for the third time: *Certain activities and categories of residency do have a liability to keep records, file forms, and pay, according to the Tax Code.* Some people are *indeed made subject* to the Tax Code, but not everyone is made subject. This means the Tax Code is constitutional, contrary to what some 'tax protestor' theories claim.

I found things that make a person into a 'taxpayer' as defined in the Internal Revenue Code; things that apparently create taxable income. In my 11 years digging around in the Tax Code, I found a number of such activities and domicile situations:

- If I live in D.C., Guam, Puerto Rico, or the Northern Mariana Islands;

- If I'm involved in manufacture or sale of alcohol, tobacco, or firearms;

- If I'm an officer or employee of the federal government;

- If I operate a merchant vessel;

- If I'm a nonresident alien or a principal of a foreign corporation with income derived from sources within the United States;

- If I'm a resident alien lawfully admitted to a State of the Union, District of Columbia, or insular possession of the United States;

- If I entered a voluntary withholding agreement for government personnel withholding either as an 'employee' (3401(c)) or an 'employer' (3401(d)) (See 26 CFR §31.3402(p)-1);

- If I've ever been notified by the Treasury Financial Management Service that I was responsible for administration of government personnel withholding (26 U.S.C. § 3403), or have applied for and received a Form 8655 Reporting Agent Authorization certificate;

- If I'm an officer or employee of the Treasury or a bureau of the Dept of Treasury subject to IRS related to submission of c o l - lected taxes delegated by Treasury Order 150-15;

- If I receive items of taxable income from foreign sources;

- If I receive foreign mineral income;

- If I receive income from foreign oil and gas extraction;

- If I receive income from a China Trade Act corporation;

- If I receive income from a foreign controlled corporation as fiduciary agent of the corporation;

- If I receive income from insurance of U.S. risks under 26 U.S.C. 953(b)(5);

- If I receive taxable items of income from operation of an a g r e e - ment vessel under section 607 of the Merchant Marine Act of 1936, as amended;

- If I receive items of income from a public works contract subject to Federal income and Social Security tax withholding;

- If I own stock in, do business with, or have anything else to with a corporation in which the [Federal] United States of America owns stock. (See notes following 18 U.S.C. § 1001. Chapter 194, 40 Stat. 1015);

- If I receive wages, remuneration, or other compensation as an officer or employee of an oceangoing vessel construed as an American employer;

- If I receive gambling winnings from the District of Columbia or insular possessions of the United States;

- If I receive items of income from maritime (international) trade in alcohol, tobacco or firearms;

- If I receive items of income from production and/or distribution of alcohol, tobacco or firearms in the District of Columbia or insular possessions of the United States;

- If I receive any items of income from activities taking place within an "internal revenue district" as such districts have been established under authority of 26 USC 7621 (Customs ports);

- If I receive items of income from maritime (international) trade in opium, cocaine or other controlled substances...

****

So many taxable activities! But I haven't found *my* line of work in there anywhere; in fact I haven't found the activities of the average American living and working in one of the 50 States.

For years, I repeatedly demanded any citation of law from IRS and from several of my representatives in Congress, that makes me a Taxpayer as defined in law. So many other activities are *treated specifically* in the Code. But year after year, I only got evasion from IRS employees and my elected scoundrels. After the first few years, my terror victim conditioning finally wore off and I've remained a happy Nontaxpayer ever since.

To reiterate for the fourth time: *the Tax Code does make some people subject to an income tax.* I just showed you a long list. But I am not on that list so I am a law-abiding, happy Nontaxpayer.

Black's Law Dictionary Agrees...

Black's Law Dictionary defines the legal principle *inclusio unius est exclusio alterius* (Latin for 'to include one is to exclude all others'):

> *Where law expressly describes a particular situation to which it shall apply, an irrefutable inference must be drawn that what is omitted or excluded was intended to be omitted or excluded.*

I listed many sections of the Code describing *'particular situations to which it shall apply'* and since I can find nothing showing that my activities are likewise taxable, an irrefutable inference must be drawn that my income is not taxable.

The U.S. Supreme Court agrees...

Keeping in mind the well-settled rule that the citizen is exempt from taxation unless the same is imposed by clear and unequivocal language, and that where the construction of a tax law is doubtful, the doubt is to be resolved in favor of those upon whom the tax is sought to be laid. **Spreckels Sugar Refining Co. v. McClain, 192 U.S. 297 (1904)**

In the interpretation of statutes levying taxes it is the established rule not to extend their provisions, by implication, beyond the clear import of the language used, or to enlarge their operations so as to embrace matters not specifically pointed out. In case of doubt they are construed most strongly against the government, and in favor of the citizen. **Gould v. Gould, 245 U.S. 151 (1917)**

In view of other settled rules of statutory construction, which teach that a law is presumed, in the absence of clear expression to the contrary, to operate prospectively; that, if doubt exists as to the construction of a taxing statute, the doubt should be resolved in favor of the taxpayer... **Hassett v. Welch., 303 US 303, 82 L Ed 858. (1938)**

Sutherland's Rules agrees...

A core text on statutory construction used by the American Bar Association, *Sutherland's Rules of Statutory Construction* is a ten-volume exhaustive resource of principles of statutory interpretation. Under the section *Strict Construction of Statutes Creating Tax*

Liability I found this, precisely in harmony with the high court rulings just noted:

> [*I*]*t is a settled rule that <u>tax laws are to be strictly construed</u> against the state and in favor of the taxpayer. Where there is reasonable doubt of the meaning of a revenue statute, the doubt is resolved in favor of those taxed. Revenue laws are considered neither remedial statutes, nor laws founded upon any public policy, and are therefore <u>not liberally construed</u>.* **Sutherland's Rules for Statutory Construction, 66:1**

The Internal Revenue Manual agrees…

Even an unsigned, computer-generated demand for money can be extortion. When I demand to see a law I'm violating or that supposedly made me owe a tax, the IRS operative must obey his operations manual and show me the law:

4.10.7.1 Overview.

> *Examiners are responsible for determining the correct tax liability as prescribed by the Internal Revenue Code. <u>It is imperative that examiners can identify the applicable law</u>, correctly interpret its meaning in light of congressional intent, and, in a fair and impartial manner, correctly apply the law based on the facts and circumstances of the case.*

4.10.7.2 Researching Tax Law.

> *Conclusions reached by examiners must reflect correct application of the law, regulations, court cases, revenue rulings, etc. Examiners must correctly determine the meaning of statutory provisions and <u>not adopt strained interpretation</u>.*

4.10.7.2.1.1 Authority of the Internal Revenue Code.

The Internal Revenue Code is generally binding on all courts of law. The courts give great importance to the literal language of the Code.

4.10.7.2.9.8 Importance of Court Decisions.

The Internal Revenue Service must follow Supreme Court decisions. For examiners, Supreme Court decisions have the same weight as the Code.

[Legal, definition, and case cites above, underline emphasis added.]

This mountain of well-settled law demands two legal and logical corollaries: a) nothing is to be presumed taxable until finding it *specifically indicated in law* as taxable; b) if *some* things are shown as taxable then things *not in the law* cannot be presumed taxable.

If a section of law actually existed showing my work as taxable, how long would that take to dig up, a *minute?* Instead, as often as I've demanded an answer from my employees at IRS, they have demonstrated a pattern of willful evasion, violating their operations manual and violating the law via attempted extortion. Passing the hot potato from one regional office to another like bullies in a playground, claiming *"we haven't finished our research; we'll get back to you."* The dog ate their homework.

Every evasive non-response I received to my certified mail demands was additional evidence that they're engaged in willful evasion of law. I have sent all correspondence to IRS via certified mail and I keep hard copies and offsite electronic backups of everything. As a former terror victim, I am cautious.

I am always factual and as firm in my responses as an employer should be when dealing with corrupt employees who work for a terror organization.

The critical tactical point is this: to reverse the cancerous growth of the corrupt socialist and fascist State, every citizen should be willing to pay any amount due by law. If that amount is zero *then I had to be willing to pay zero* because only by starving corruption will we bring government back within the limits set by the Constitution.

Criminals at IRS are posing as enforcement officers

I doubt that chasing thugs is a wise use of time, but if I had wanted to go after extortionists at IRS just for fun, I'd have begun by using this section of the Tax Code, since their manual says they must show the law under which they're trying to shake me down for cash. If they can't show the law, they're committing *extortion:*

Section 7214(a)
Offenses by officers and employees of the United States

Any officer or employee of the United States acting in connection with any revenue law of the United States (1) who is guilty of any extortion or willful oppression under color of law; or (2) who knowingly demands other or greater sums than are authorized by law ... upon conviction thereof shall be fined not more than $10,000 or imprisoned not more than 5 years, or both.

You are Hereby SUMMONED (...by Muffy the cat...)

Once I learned not to fear scary letterhead not backed by law, the fraudsters started looking silly. I learned that an IRS 'summons' is of no legal consequence as a federal court ruled in 2005:

> *...absent an effort to seek enforcement through a federal court, IRS summonses apply no force to taxpayers, and no consequence whatever can befall a taxpayer who refuses, ignores, or otherwise does not comply with an IRS summons until that summons is backed by a federal court order... [a taxpayer] cannot be held in contempt, arrested, detained, or otherwise punished for refusing to comply with the original IRS summons, no matter*

the taxpayer's reasons, or lack of reasons for so complying. **U.S. 2nd Appellate Court- Schulz v. IRS (2005)**

I could gain a 4-count indictment on IRS Thugs

Here in Texas we have it best of all. Texas law stipulates that it's a criminal offense every time the IRS sends a supposed 'summons' or anything else that can be construed by the citizen as originating from the judicial branch; that's the first criminal count for an indictment:

Texas Penal Code
CHAPTER 32. FRAUD
32.48. SIMULATING LEGAL PROCESS.

> *(a) A person commits an offense if the person recklessly causes to be delivered to another any document that simulates a summons, complaint, judgment, or other court process with the intent to: (1) induce payment of a claim from another person; or (2) cause another to: (A) submit to the putative authority of the document; or (B) take any action or refrain from taking any action in response to the document, in compliance with the document, or on the basis of the document. (e) Except as provided by Subsection (f), an offense under this section is a Class A misdemeanor. (f) If it is shown on the trial of an offense under this section that the defendant has previously been convicted of a violation of this section, the offense is a state jail felony.*

The laws of Texas provide for a second count on the criminal indictment of IRS employees when they filed a 'Notice of Federal Tax Lien' in our Texas county records. As I learned, it was no legal lien at all. It was just teams of administrative employees, committing fraud by their manager's orders:

Texas Government Code
51.901. FRAUDULENT DOCUMENT OR INSTRUMENT.

(c)For purposes of this section, a document or instrument is presumed to be fraudulent if: ...(2) the document or instrument purports to create a lien or assert a claim against real or personal property or an interest in real or personal property and: ... (B) is not created by implied or express consent or agreement of the obligor, debtor, or the owner of the real or personal property... (C) is not an equitable, constructive, or other lien imposed by a court with jurisdiction created or established under the constitution or laws of this state or of the United States.

Although it was not technically harming me, the IRS employees refused to play ball and get that NFTL fraud out of my county records since 2004, so Texas law gives me a *third* count for a criminal indictment against the agency:

Texas Penal Code
CHAPTER 32. FRAUD.

32.49. Refusal to execute release of fraudulent lien or claim.
(a) A person commits an offense if, with intent to defraud or harm another, the person:(1) owns, holds, or is the beneficiary of a purported lien or claim asserted against real or personal property or an interest in real or personal property that is fraudulent, as described by Section 51.901(c), Government Code; and (2) not later than the 21st day after the date of receipt of actual or written notice sent by either certified or registered mail, return receipt requested, to the person's last known address, or by telephonic document transfer to the recipient's current telecopier number, requesting the execution of a release of the fraudulent lien or claim, refuses to execute the release on the request of: (A) the obligor or debtor; (B) any person who owns any interest in the real or personal property described in the document or

instrument that is the basis for the lien or claim. (b) <u>A person</u> <u>*who fails to execute a release of the purported lien or claim*</u> <u>*within the period prescribed by Subsection (a)(2) is presumed to*</u> <u>*have had the intent to harm or defraud another.*</u> *(c) An offense under this section is a Class A misdemeanor.*

Thus under Texas law, IRS commits a crime every time it files a 'Notice of Federal Tax Lien' against a Texan. If a court didn't issue a judgment, then no lien can exist. Period. *A notice is not a lien.* No one is above the law in America!

I'm not suggesting anyone try to pursue federal mafia in a state court. I'm simply illustrating that in Texas law, we Texans have the right and power to pursue bent federal actors in our state courts.

Bankers and mortgage companies in Texas should know the law. Instead, they violate their fiduciary duty to customers, and usually help the IRS terrorize them. Of course I'm sure it's usually out of fear or ignorance because we all know how honest the and diligent the banking and mortgage industries are. And of course, IRS operatives have an excuse too, like the prison guards at Auschwitz. They're just following orders from Congress.

You've seen the provisions from the Tax Code and the Internal Revenue Manual. Ignorance of the law is no excuse for serial fraud and terrorism by IRS employees.

The fourth fraud count on the criminal indictment I can ask the Grand Jury for is the IRS *team signature* fraud. After looking at almost a dozen examples of a Notice of Federal Tax Lien, I discovered one more IRS fraud tactic: every NFTL is signed in ink by *one* person using only first initial, and a *second* person's full printed name appears below the signature. Is their up-line manager covering their tails in case they're caught, so that both operatives can deny having filed the fraudulent lien by just blaming the other?

Incidentally, not all judges are corrupt. The U.S. Supreme Court had this to say about government employees defrauding citizens:

This is the approach that has been taken by each of the Courts of Appeals that has addressed the issue: schemes to defraud include those designed to deprive individuals, the people...of intangible rights such as the right to have public officials perform their duties honestly. **McNally v. United States 483 U.S. (1987) at 358**

If I hadn't begun reading law and digging for facts, I would have been defrauded all my working life. Instead, I've made copies of everything so as to be able to prove to the average jury what Congress demands of IRS, and how it trains its employees as racketeers and terrorist operatives.

I knew that before they could take any of my stuff, the crooks had to file that bogus 'lien notice'. I filed a public complaint right away when IRS tried to steal from me that way.

I filed an *Affidavit of Material Facts* (sample at the blog article below) with our county clerk.

http://taxhonestyprimer.blogspot.com/2010/02/affidavit-of-material-facts.html

Every point in a signed, notarized affidavit that is not specifically answered is established in the record. Since then, I've been on the record that I only signed as 'Taxpayer' under penalty of perjury all those years out of ignorance and coercion.

Since then, I've informed my clients and my bank's attorney that filing an NFTL is a criminal act in Texas. I sent my bank a certified letter informing them that if IRS claims funds in my account without a judge's ruling, I'll demand my full deposits from the bank just as if any other criminal stole my funds on deposit.

Americans must not remain terror victims; no American should *ever* fear his public servants. Your government can only use terror to make you pay its demands as long as you're uninformed and subservient to those who took an oath to serve *you*.

The FairTax is a Trojan horse

Remember what Tax Honesty is about: money *and liberty.* The fraudsters in Congress have had the 'FairTax' scam waiting in the wings for over a decade; potentially an even worse scam than the one we're finally busting and most importantly it would continue to let Congress collect five times more revenues than are required for its lawful functions. America would leap from the frying pan into the fire under the promise of 'getting rid of the IRS'. *It's a lie.*

Reading is critical in our day

Besides the Tax Code and resources mentioned above, I recommend the *Suggested Reading* section. Learn how long this battle has been raging; you never learned real history!

The generation of Marx, Darwin, and Lincoln was America's watershed into tyranny. What most believe began in 1913 was brewing in the dens, offices, and clubs of powerful men for 80 years before Wilson's corrupt administration and the gangsters from Jekyll Island.

American history is fascinating; if we learn its lessons, perhaps we'll stop being condemned to repeat them.